BONE AND HORN CARVING

Also by Carson I. A. Ritchie

Modern Ivory Carving
Shell Carving

BONE AND HORN CARVING

A Pictorial History

Carson I.A. Ritchie

South Brunswick and New York: A. S. Barnes and Company
London: Thomas Yoseloff Ltd

A. S. Barnes and Co., Inc.
Cranbury, New Jersey 08512

Thomas Yoseloff Ltd
108 New Bond Street
London W1Y OQX, England

Library of Congress Cataloging in Publication Data

Ritchie, Carson I A
Bone and horn carving.

Includes bibliographical references.
1. Bone carving. 2. Horn carving. I. Title.
NK6020.R52 736′.6 73-22601
ISBN 0-498-01404-5

PRINTED IN THE UNITED STATES OF AMERICA

Mainline 2.78

CONTENTS

ACKNOWLEDGMENTS

It is a pleasure to acknowledge all the help I have received in writing this book. Mrs. Willson Pemberton and Mrs. Eva Bluth helped me to cope with what appeared to be insuperable language problems. Mr. Boston of the Horniman Museum was extremely helpful. Mr. Hugh Moss gave me much invaluable advice. I also owe a considerable debt of gratitude to Mr. Bob Hall of Hugh M. Moss Ltd., Oriental Works of Art, 12 Bruton St., London. I should also like to thank Mr. Swain of the Commonwealth Institute, Mr. B. Newbury of the Parker Gallery, Sotheby & Co., Mrs. Drey of New York (Paul Drey Gallery), the staff and the Press Officer at Christies, and Mr. John Herbert. My thanks are particularly due to the Director of the London Museum and to Mrs. Christine Waters.

INTRODUCTION

Few substances have left such an impress on the art of the world as bone and horn. They were mankind's earliest art materials, and, not surprisingly, most of the masterpieces of very early times were executed in them. Bone and horn can be easily dissolved by acid solutions, such as our digestive juices, a fact which the great British surgeon, Sir Astley Cooper, demonstrated visually for the first time by painting the names of famous medical men on bones in acid-resisting paint. After a period of digestion in a dog's stomach it was only the painted name which still stood out in relief. Where natural solvents are not present and where bone objects are not destroyed by fire, they are well nigh imperishable. We know a lot about many periods of the world's art, such as that of the ancient men of the Arctic, because objects made in bone have survived, while others have perished.

Not only did the bone and horn materials used during very early periods leave us a permanent record of early art, they are materials which have been in constant use throughout history, unlike paper, for example. Though it may not, at present, be experiencing its greatest days, bone and horn carving is still a living craft, unlike so many others which have disappeared.

Bone has a special importance in that it is a sketch book material in which early artists tended to make a record of fugitive impressions. It also under-pinned many of the other arts, such as those of the jeweller and metal worker. It was in bone, a material near in hardness to bullion though softer than it, that the jeweller and metal worker learned to carve the patterns that they would later carve in gold and silver. Bone may also have been important as a pattern material, from which the patterns for molds were carved.

Horn, too, has always occupied a very special place. Its shape designated its use as a container, for liquids, and, as we shall see later, for gunpowder as well. It is no accident that the great days of horn carving were those when its function as a container and as a natural musical instrument were well to the fore. Horn was also one of the few plastics which medieval craftworkers had at their disposal. Hence it came to be used for a variety of purposes where plasticity was important, making spoons for example. Because it could be easily cleaned, and was grease-repellent, it found many other uses, such as making combs (for which bone was also used), and for knife handles. Whalebone and horn were very useful all-purpose materials for the medieval craftsmen. Knights had their tournament helmet plumes made from whalebone, which would deflect a blow because of its springiness. The monks of Durham in Northumberland, England, used baleen-handled pen knives to trim their quill pens, and attached them to charters instead of seals, as a testimony. The odorlessness of horn later caused it to be used for pressing out snuffbox lids by the seventeenth-century London craftsman Obrisset. It was important that the carefully balanced flavor of the snuff should not be upset by any taint or odor from the container in which it was carried.

Like most substances with an important history, bone and horn had strong magical associations. Scottish witches used cursing bones, many of which have survived. Aleutian sorcerers tore away a fragment from the jaw of a mummified wizard and kept it in their mouths so that the power of their predecessor would be conveyed to them. Whereas bone was a relic of what was left once the spirit had departed, horn was very much associated with the affairs of this world. It was the symbol of male potency. Animals and birds which bore horns as a highly developed secondary sexual characteristic, such as the rhinoceros and the hornbill, became sought after as the providers, not just of raw material for carvings, but of sexual sufficiency in the owners of such carvings. Along with the glamour they received as aphrodisiacs, some horns also began to be looked on as prophylactics. This was particularly true of the rhinoceros horn, which was credited with the power of exuding a white effervescence in the presence of poison.

Although some bones and horns were very exotic and difficult to come by, such as the jaguar's bones, carved by the Mixtecs, most bone and horn was virtually waste material. The powder horns of nineteenth-century America were imported duty-free from the West Indies, Mexico, and South America, by the firm of Bird, tanners of Dorchester near Boston, because horns were classified as scrap. Bone and horn thus acquire a special importance in that they are a poor man's material, created specially for the folk artist, with more ideas and talent than money. So some of the finest carvings in bone (carvings that would rank with those made in any other material) were made by sculptors who did not have a penny to bless themselves with, such as the American prisoners of war in British camps during the war of 1812. Do not forget, when we come to assess these carvings, that they were made, literally, with prisoners' flesh and blood, because any part of a bone model or toy could have been eaten, if boiled long enough. American prisoners on Dartmoor had early evolved a method of reducing the hardest bone to a nourishing jelly. Many prisoners asserted that a diet of this jelly kept them healthy as well as adding to their scanty rations. As it is rich in calcium, it would of course have a tonic effect on them.

The other famous set of folk artists, who worked in bone because they could afford nothing else, were, of course, the scrimshoners. Working in the cramped quarters of a Nantucket whaler, they created the first important American art form, one which was to be eagerly bought by Europeans in special shops in France, Europeans who perhaps would not have been a bit impressed by work done by professional American artists or sculptors. Bone and horn carving are very democratic arts, in which the humble can often confound the proud, as did the anonymous and lowly monks who labored at *alla certosina* work in the convents of Italy. It is true that it has taken a long time for the efforts of the scrimshoners to be appreciated at their true worth. Even now unthinking people speak about it as being "crude" or "rough", but they would not be so prone to criticize it if they had to do it themselves, by the light of a flickering sludge lamp in the foc'sle of a whaler pitching to and fro off the Japanese archipelago, with no better tool than a pickwick which kept sticking itself into their finger instead of the whalebone.

This brings up the practical side of bone and horn carving. I have spoken about horn and bone carving as though they were one and the same, while in fact they are very different. This difference is caused by the fact that bone and horn are two very dissimilar substances. Bone is the hard material which makes up animal skeletons; it is made up of gelatine and phosphate of lime, together with some carbonate of lime, phosphate of magnesia, and soda. The only bones which offer a solid, consistent substance to carve are flat bones, like the shoulder blades. Long or marrow bones, such as thigh bones, have a hollow spongy interior; virtually all that can be done with a long bone is to saw off both ends, slice it down the middle, and try and find as much carving surface as possible on the rounded panels thus obtained. Of course, the larger the animal which provided it, the larger the surface which will be yielded by a piece of bone. It is, then, not surprising that many of the great carvings of the world were made on whalebone. It was only this material which gave the bold and ambitious sculptor, such as the carver of the Whalebone Madonna, enough scope.

One of the interesting features of bone is that it is easily confused with ivory. Both are hard and white, and both sometimes appear together in the same object, because the craftsman who carved one might well carve the other as well. An object made in one substance may be patched in another—a snuff bottle made in hornbill, for example, might be fitted with a new neck in ivory. It is not always possible to distinguish one substance from another without a very close examination, particularly if the surface has become stained or acquired a patina. When quite new, bone is marked with thin black lines or flecks, but is otherwise a unified white. Ivory is either an all-color creamy white, or yellow-striped by white striations. However, some kinds of ivory, such as hippopotamus ivory or narwhal ivory, exhibit strange mottlings and flecks which can be confused with those of bone.

A natural consequence of this similarity is that museum curators and art historians are constantly confusing the two substances. Carvings labeled in one generation as 'ivory" have become "bone" in the next. Sculptures described in books are frequently bone when they are described as ivory, and vice versa. One famous carving in the Metropolitan Museum in New York is described as "bone" on the caption of a plate, and "ivory" in the notes. Although many writers are subject to this kind of error, those who are in the greatest state of confusion about bone and ivory are the Russians. Whenever a Russian, whether writing in his own language or translated into English, writes about "bone carving," there is a very good chance that he really means "ivory carving." I shall try to account for this confusion later.

Just because the two substances are often mixed up, a study of bone carving throws great light, not merely on ivory carving, but on our own ideas about aesthetics. Would we like an ivory carving just as much if we discovered that it was really a bone carving? If we feel disappointed to learn that a supposed ivory carving is bone, then we may be attaching too much importance to the material, and not enough to the artist who fashions it.

Horn is a modified form of epidermic tissue, and consists of the albuminoid keratin. Because the molecules in keratin can be restructured, it is possible to melt horn in the heat of a charcoal fire or in boiling water, and press it in a mold. Although called horns, the antlers of deer are really bone, while those of the rhinoceros are made up of horny matter in the form of long bristles compressed into a cone shape. Whalebone is the term applied either to the bones of the whale, particularly its jawbone, or more usually, though incorrectly, to the baleen, a black horny substance which lines the mouths of some species of whales.

Horn and bone have had a very long history as useful as well as artistic materials, and often artistry must have arisen among workmen who fashioned tools and weapons for everyday use. It is probably not accidental that the ancient Parthians, famous for the unerring aim with which they discharged arrows from their composite bows made from horn and other materials, also carved fine bone plaques, or that frontier America, where a man kept as close as possible to his rifle and powder horn, evolved scrimshaw as we know it today.

Unique in many other respects, bone and horn carving are also unsurpassed in the interest of their associations. Just to look at a carved medieval horn makes one think of the Battle of Hastings, and how the Norman minstrel Taillefer put new heart into his comrades, wavering at the sight of the English shield wall, by singing to them about Roland and his horn. A carved snuff bottle of hornbill conjures up quite different associations; it evokes a picture of the Punan, stalking the gorgeous bird through the forests of Borneo, with his eight foot long blowpipe raised to his lips, and two darts, each tipped with the poison of the Ipoh tree, tucked behind his ears. Few art objects can be so provocative of thought as the ships of despair rigged by American prisoners, or the trophies of hand to hand combat with the greatest animal in the world ornamented by the American scrimshoner. Humble-seeming in substance, bone and horn are rich in lore, in legend, and in the artistic genius lavished upon them.

BONE AND HORN CARVING

1
METHOD AND FORM

ARE the artistic forms which bone and horn have taken over the past millenia solely those imposed by the artist, or has the material itself dictated the shapes which bone and horn carving should assume? We may be better able to answer these questions by examining, very shortly, some of the techniques which the bone and horn carver employs. Man only does what he can, and the success of bone carving has been determined, by and large, by the practical skills employed. Where they have been wanting or limited the results have generally been disappointing, but where technique has flourished, superb artistry has often resulted. Not infrequently, the transition from complete incompetence to superb technique has been a very rapid one. An American prisoner of war in England during the War of 1812 pointed out that most of his fellow prisoners had never shaped a piece of bone in their lives. However, the necessity of earning a living in a community where only the bare necessities of life were supplied and where all luxuries (such as tobacco and coffee) had to be bought very soon turned many of them into bone sculptors of consummate artistry, as a glance at some of their work will show.

Although I have tried to emphasize the practical side to sculpture in bone and horn, I would be the first to admit that my knowledge of techniques is very limited and incomplete. Anyone who writes about bone carving is bound to experience the same limitations that I have. Our knowledge of practical skills in this art has been restricted in part by the fact that some bone workers were very keen to keep their work methods secret. The crossbow makers of Barcelona circulated the most improbable stories—which will be recounted later in the book—about the source of the raw material from which their bows were made. It is more usual, however, that travelers and writers have been too incurious about practical methods of work to give us an account of them. There are of course, exceptions to this rule. Charles G. Leland, an English clergyman who wrote innumerable works on craft during the 1880s, and who is not to be confused with the much more famous American C. G. Leland, the Etruscologist, was a dedicated collector of receipts and work methods. He had taken lessons in inlaying bone and exotic woods, in the manner of the Embriachis, which will be described later, from "old Hassan, a Cairene inlayer."[1] He had also

1. Charles Godfrey Leland, *The Minor Arts* (London, 1880), p. 135.

watched South American sailors and gauchos ornamenting ox horns with a hot iron or with sulphuric acid. Moreover, he had assiduously researched into British crafts. Even now a certain amount of horn carving is carried out in Britain. Shepherds in the Highlands of Scotland often carry horn-handled walking sticks or crooks, called *cromachs,* and many minor products, such as spoons and cups, are still made of horn. In Leland's time horn and bone working were much more extensive than they are now, so he is a good authority on how such work was carried out.

Talking of horn work, he comments that horns may be etched by coating them with wax or varnish, scratching out the pattern, and then pouring acid and water on them. They can also have a pattern designed on them with ink, and then have the pattern chiseled in with a small, sharp V-shaped tool. Finally, the lines of the design will be picked out in ink, or dye, with a fine camel hair brush. Horn, he goes on to say, can be flattened by steeping it for some time in hot water. In fact, it can be made perfectly plastic, and molded into any shape that is required. Horns are polished, first with sand paper, next with powdered pumice and water, and finally with fine whiting and water. Stiff brushes applied the polishing powders, and the final shine was imparted with a piece of leather glued to a stick.

Whereas horn was a very versatile material which could be split, pressed, molded, rendered transparent, and dyed, bone was a much more straightforward substance. Nevertheless, Gordon Stables, another Victorian authority on craft, pointed out that the shaping and polishing methods for horn and bone were almost exactly the same. Bones were pared, scraped, and rubbed with knives, sandpaper, and a variety of abrasives and polishes, such as tripoli, jeweler's rouge, and putty powder. Like horns, bones could readily be dyed into a wide variety of colors.

Leland and Stables wrote for an unskilled audience. Stables wrote particularly for schoolboys. There was nothing in horn and bone work which was too difficult for anyone with a little determination, persistence, and enthusiasm to carry out. Sculpture in these two materials bore the same relation to sculpture in different substances, such as stone or bronze, that drawing with a pencil does to painting a picture in oils. There is little wonder, then, that, as I remarked in the Introduction, bone and horn carving have always been an ordinary man's art, something that anyone could do if he had any artistic spirt in him, and something that everyone could afford to make and to buy. Because bone and horn carving are largely a folk art, and the folk artist has less leisure to complete his task than his professional counterpart, the form of the material was all-important. The forms of horns and bones have often dictated the shapes of objects made in the past (and sometimes still in use today) such as knife handles, for example. By and large, bones admitted of only flat or tubular shapes—all the more credit then, to the American prisoner artist who conjured them into full-rigged ships. Scrimshaw came to the fore as an art form largely because it was easier to inscribe pictures on a flat bone surface than carve it into shapes. Bone shapes were often dictated by a desire to make something which looked like ivory, horn shapes sometimes imitated those of tortoiseshell. The very cheapness and abundance of the material, however, prompted experimentation and a ceaseless striving for new effects.

2

PUT YOUR TRUST IN GOD AND KEEP YOUR POWDER DRY.

American Folk Carving

ONE of the charms of the seventeenth century is that it contains, in embryo, a lot which will only reach its full stature much later. Just as the germ of America itself lay hidden in the meetings of an obscure sect in the house of a village postmaster in Yorkshire, so the origins of what was later to be American scrimshaw were carried ashore at Plymouth by the Pilgrim Fathers. They had learned by bitter experience that however good one's intentions may be (theirs were of the best) it takes two to keep the peace. So the first sixteen of the Pilgrims went ashore fully armed, carrying with them the engraved powder horns used in contemporary England, which along with the engraved horn tobacco boxes of Stuart times, were to provide the inspiration for scrimshaw.

The first powder flasks had appeared about a century before the Pilgrims landed. They can be seen in contemporary engravings, such as a picture of a German infantryman loading his matchlock. To the men of the Renaissance, the horn was a natural, all-purpose receptacle. When it was found that Bedlam Hospital, in London, was not big enough to contain all the mentally afflicted of Tudor England, the more harmless lunatics among the inmates were given a badge licensing them to beg, and a horn, They went through the countryside, blowing their horn to implore charity, and if charity was forthcoming they put a stopper in the mouthpiece of the horn so that they could convert it into a beer mug.

A horn was an ideal receptacle for powder: it was cheap, it had a natural curve which would fit snugly into the shape of the buttock when it was worn over the shoulders and it could be pulled well behind the shooter so that none of the sparks from his gun fell into it. The narrow end of the horn acted as a natural funnel for pouring powder into the muzzle of the gun. Horns had long been used for feeding babies, and old men who had lost all their teeth. This may have suggested their use as funnels for pouring gunpowder. Horns were showerproof, and transparent, so that a glance would show you how much powder you had left.

Right from the start, horns were ornamented with elaborate designs and inscriptions. This decoration was for practical as well as for ar-

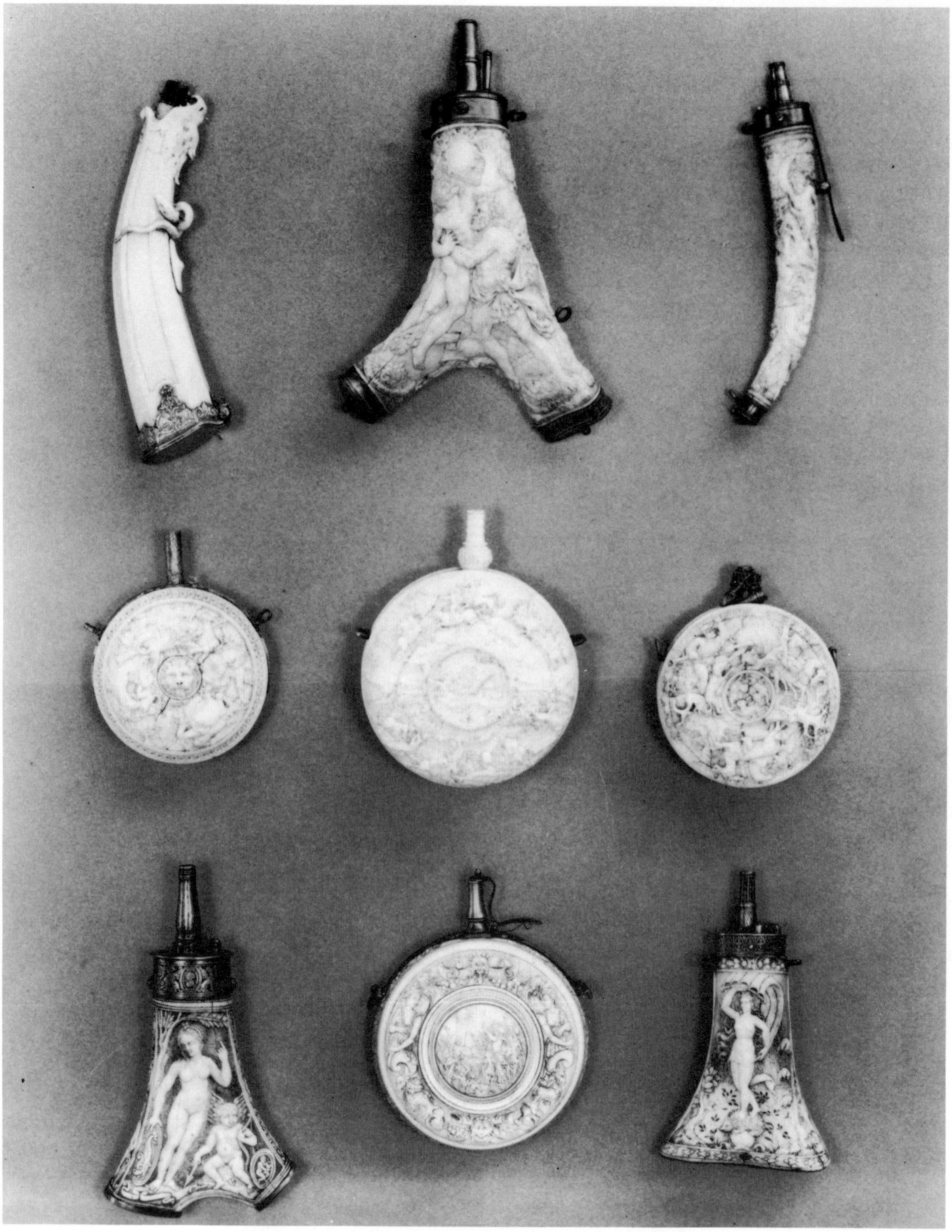

A collection of powder flasks, the middle row of ivory, (suggesting that Renaissance horn carvers were often ivory carvers as well). These flasks, which are German, Italian, and French, are all of the sixteenth century. *Courtesy Wallace Collection, London, England.*

Powder flask of walnut, inlaid with a representation of Tobias and the Angel in stag's horn, the background filled in with flowers and birds. German, about 1630, probably made by a gun stocker. *Courtesy Wallace Collection, London, England.*

Sixteenth-century French powder flask made from stag's horn, showing Samson fighting with the lion. Dated 1574. *Courtesy Victoria and Albert Museum, London, England.*

tistic reasons; one horn looks very like another and if there were a lot of them hanging up in one place it was essential that your horn should bear such a distinguishing mark so that you could pick it out straight away, and walk off with it before someone else did. Many colonial American horns bear inscriptions threatening vengeance on anyone who steals them.

From the very beginning, as I have said, horns were the subject of very elaborate decoration. An Italian horn of 1560, in the Metropolitan Museum in New York, has engraved on it a ship on a stormy sea, a castle, a forest, pastoral scenes, battles, and the gods of the ancients. Horns were an obvious outlet for the folk artist. The raw material for a horn cost virtually nothing, and all that it needed was skill and patience to make it into a really attractive possession for oneself, or present for a friend, such as the horn which Robert Minchum made for William Morris in 1601. Horns ornamented by folk artists were so attractive that people felt that a professional artist would do even better in decorating them, and at least twenty-five professional engravers were at work in America during the Colonial period.

From this native school of horn artists, scrimshaw was to evolve, not before the American artists had undergone influences, partly from horns engraved by professional craftsmen in England and carried overseas by English troops serving in America, and partly from Highland horns, brought out by Scottish soldiers. These horns form a folk art school in their own right. In the seventeenth century Scottish horn carving had undergone a minor renaissance, part of the larger movement which was called the "Celtic Revival." Beautiful handles were carved for the dirks, or long daggers, which the Highlanders carried in the inside of their shields, at their belts, or down the backs of their necks if they were travelling anywhere where arms were not usually worn. Intricate knotwork ornamented these dirk handles and the handles of the *sgean dhu* or black knife, a smaller version of the dirk worn in the top of the Highland stocking.

The interlacing patterns which ornamented these weapon handles were derived from the whalebone carvings of the fifteenth and sixteenth centuries, such as those cut on the Eglinton Casket and the Fife Casket. Ultimately, their inspiration came from the tombs of the Highland chieftains, laid to rest in Iona and elsewhere. The horns from which these carvings were made could have been trophies, not of the chase, but of the inroads which the Highlanders made regularly on the more settled Lowlands of Scotland. The word "blackmail" was coined to describe the protection money paid by Lowland estate owners to the Highland Rustlers, or "reivers" as they called themselves, after the Scots word for rent, "mail."

A typical Highland powder horn was made from a horn of a long-horned bull, boiled to soften it, and then flattened. It was finished by attaching slings for a cord which would suspend it from the owner's shoulder and fitting it with a mouthpiece stopper of wood.

The most elaborately ornamented horns were carved all over. Others, the less pretentious ones carried by simple clansmen, would be engraved. Occasionally horns destined for chiefs were engraved instead of being carved, such as that carried by Sir George M'Kenzie of Tarbat, who became baronet in 1654. His powder horn bears engravings of hunting scenes on one side, simple knotwork decoration on the other. Many of these horns are dated, which makes it easy to follow their progress from the commencement of the Celtic Revival in the seventeenth century, till its degeneracy in the eighteenth. By the latter century several types of horns had developed. They included those decorated with concentric circles, enclosing Celtic designs, those which carried coats of arms and supporters, those covered with cross-bands of knotwork and fan ornament, those ornamented with flowers, such as the Scots thistle, the English rose, and the Dutch tulip, which had come in with William of Orange in 1689, those decorated with hunting scenes, and those engraved with pictures of ships. It was from this last kind of horn, which was always unflattened, and probably dated from the eighteenth century, that the

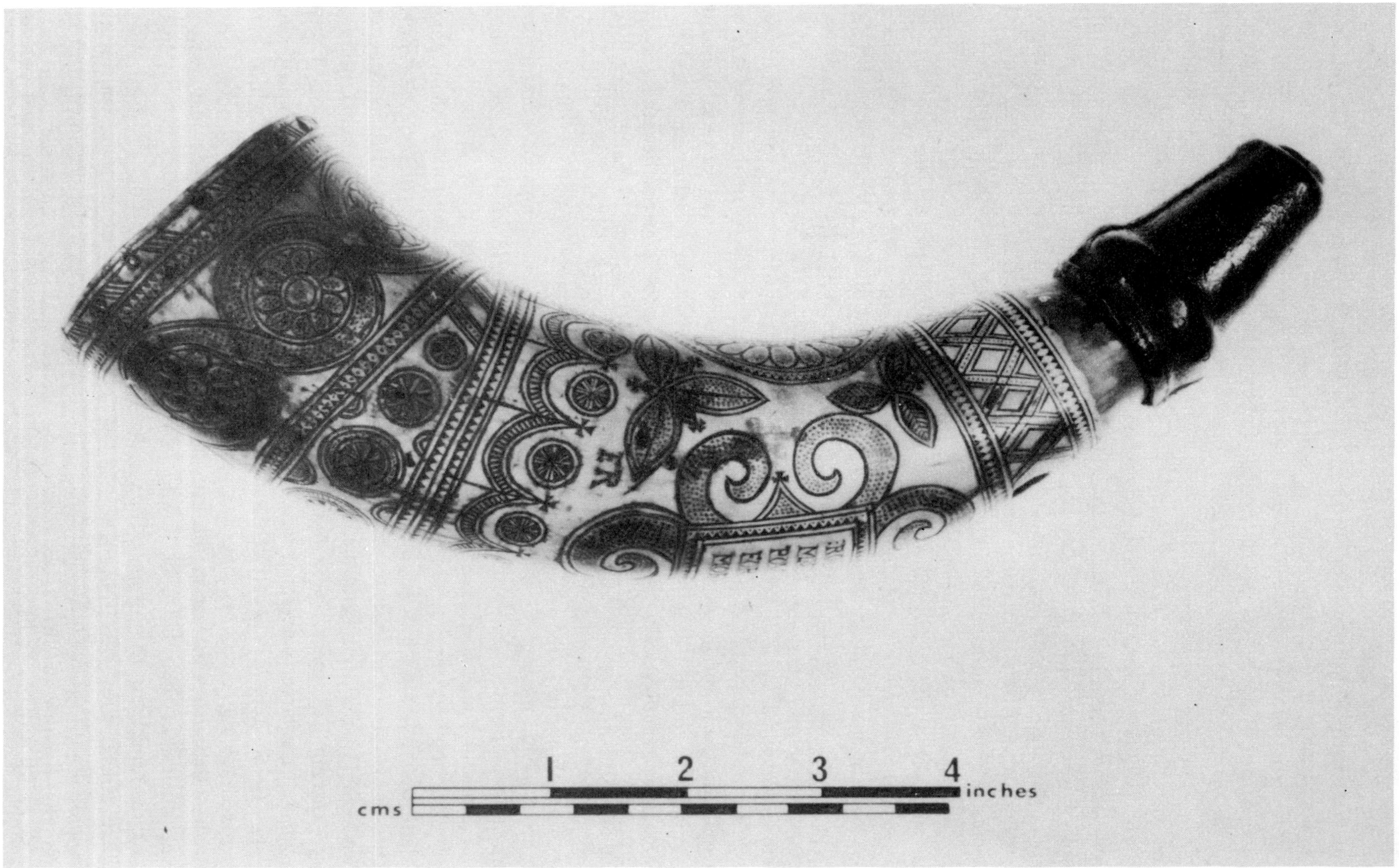

Powder flask made by Robert Mindum, in 1601, for William Morris. *Courtesy London Museum, Kensington Palace, London, England.*

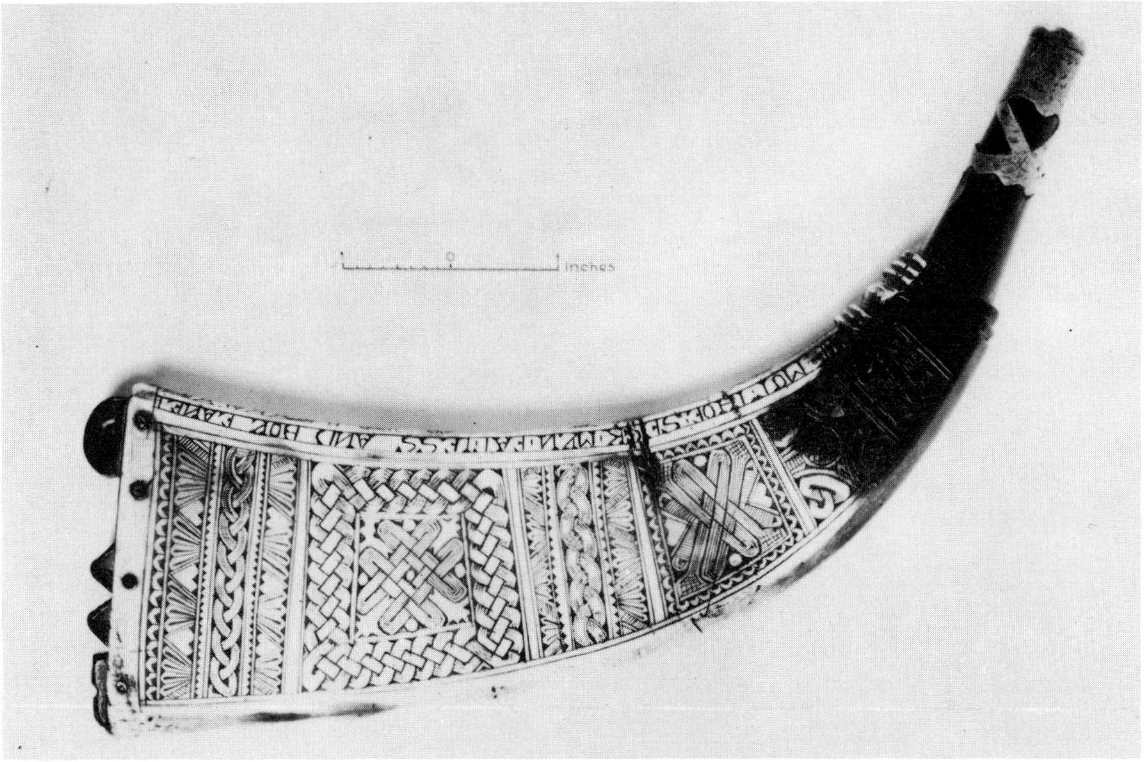

Celtic strap work is combined on this Highland powder horn with the cryptic motto: "Ill Mot Thoe Seck Myn Eat Less And Boy Eane Finis." *Courtesy National Museum of Antiquities, Scotland.*

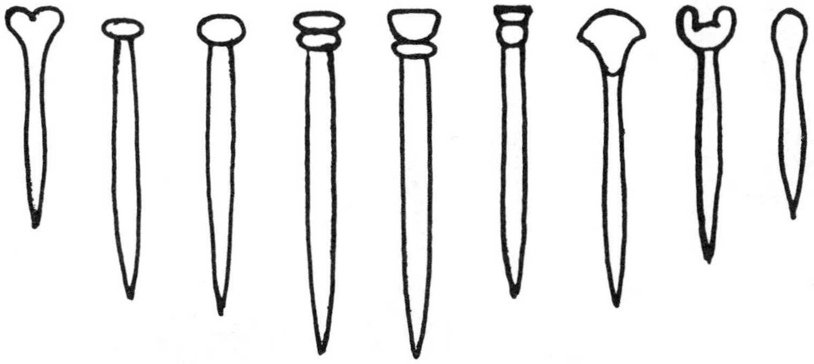

Bone pins with ornamental heads. Scotland.

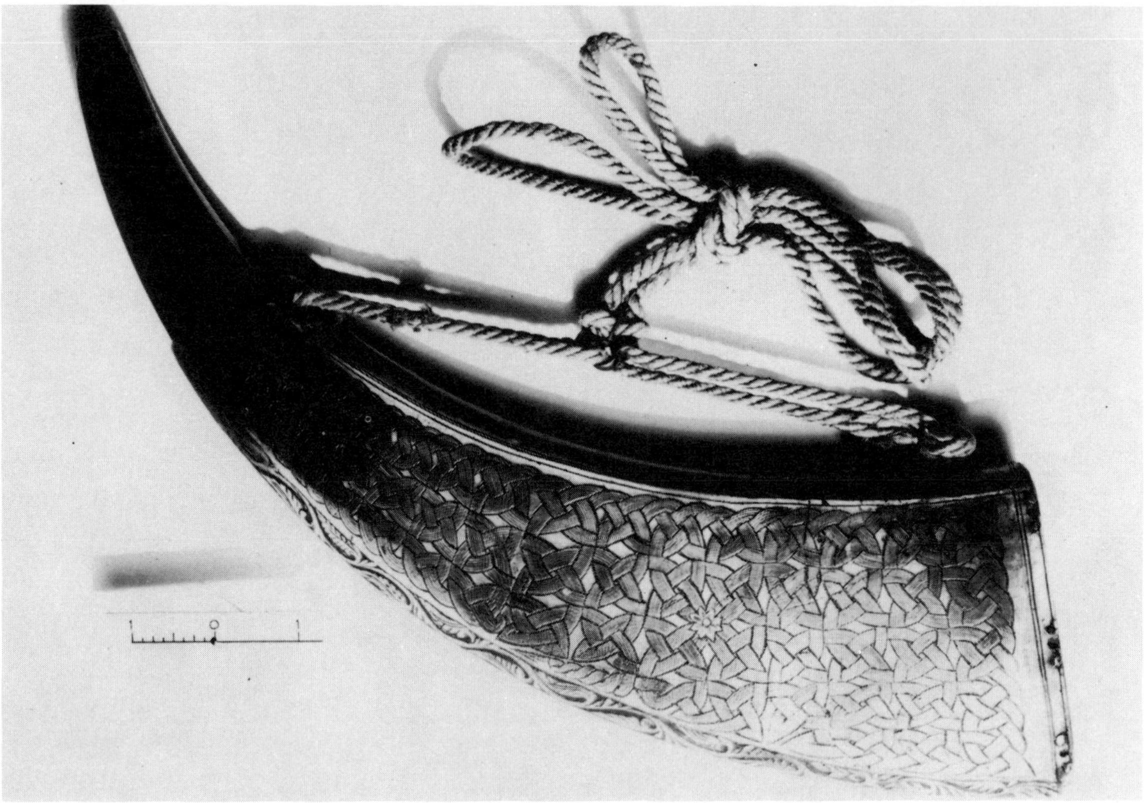

Celtic revival Highland Scottish powder horn, which belonged to M'Kenzie of Tarbat. Note the interlacing strapwork. *Courtesy National Museum of Antiquities, Scotland.*

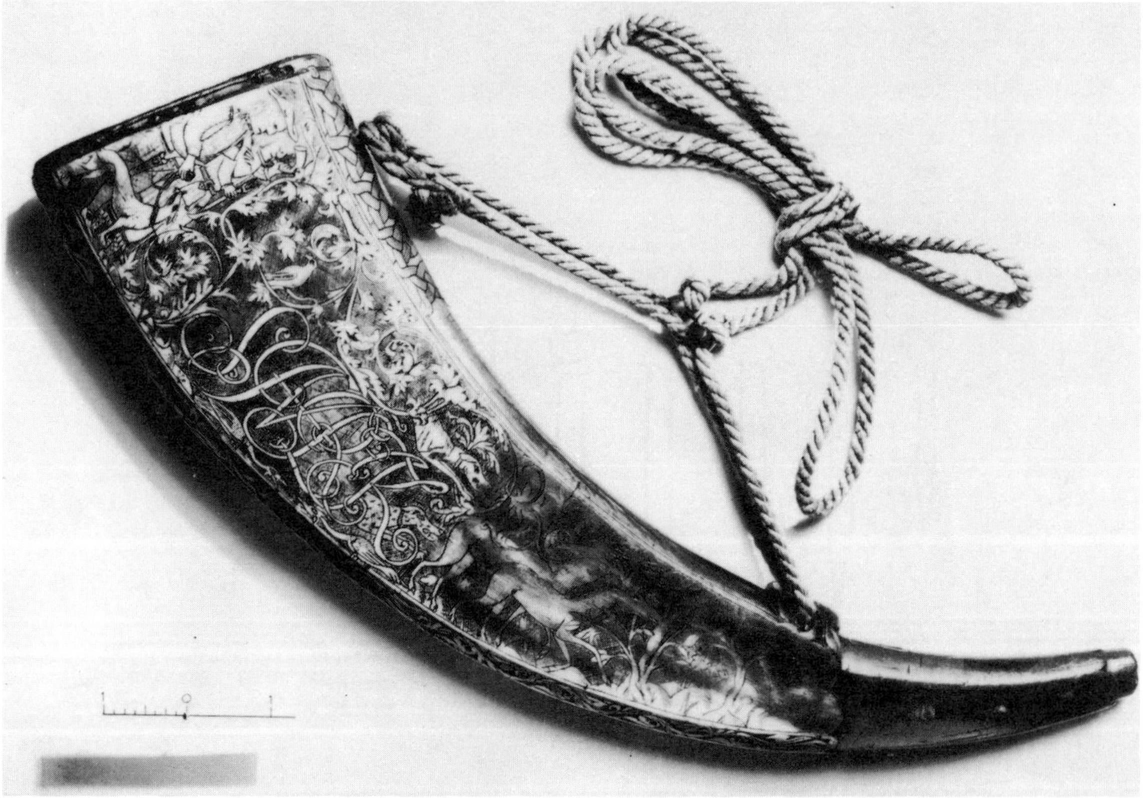

Another view of the M'Kenzie of Tarbat powder horn. Celtic ornament was combined with folk art ornament much more reminiscent of Europe than of Scotland. *Courtesy National Museum of Antiquities, Scotland.*

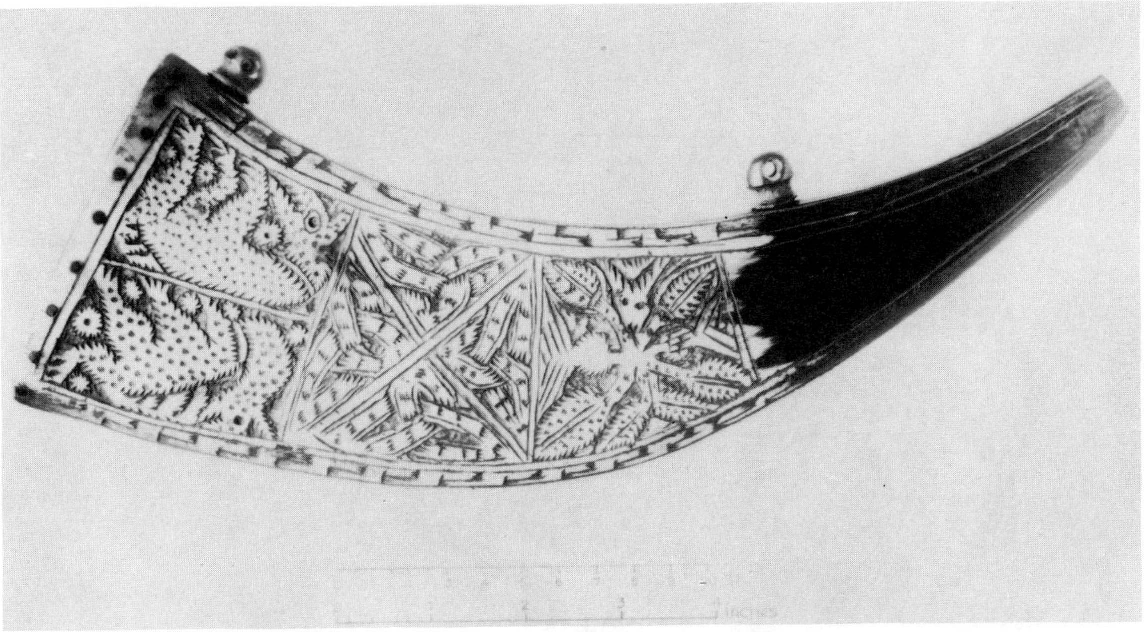

The originality of the Highland powder horn maker is seen in this horn, ornamented with strange animals. ***Courtesy National Museum of Antiquities, Scotland.***

original idea of scrimshaw, which is so concerned with pictures of ships, may have developed. Whitelaw, a Scottish art historian, felt that this kind of horn was actually meant for use at sea. If he is correct, then these horns are not so much engraved powder flasks as eighteenth-century Scottish scrimshaw.

It is quite possible that by trying to relate American horn engraving to either Scottish or English folk art I am trying to find too local a source for its inspiration. Horn decoration was a very international art. It is very difficult to be sure where the decorative elements of a folk art originate. In Hungary during the eighteenth century, for example, powder horns were made by the herdsmen on the Great Plain. The decorations of these horns, which portray the lives of the herdsmen themselves, are not unlike contemporary English hornwork and scrimshaw. The herdsmen also made bugle horns, drinking horns, salt cellars, and ointment cases. Certain of the engraved motifs have been traced back to the Renaissance styles in embroideries, church paintings and furniture ornamentation. The stag-horn powder horns have an even older style of ornamentation, which is supposed to have originated in the seventeenth-century period of the Great Migration, and which is supposed to have been originally magical. Certain of these motifs may have been carried to America, as were those other characteristically Hungarian types of military ornament, the pelisse and tall hat of the hussar, originally the dress of the Hungarian shepherd.

1745 saw the beginning of hard times for the Highlands. The Highlander followers of Bonnie Prince Charlie were defeated and massacred at Culloden. Proscriptions sent many Highlanders overseas to America as settlers, and they were soon followed by Highland regiments, enlisted by prime minister Pitt to fight the French and Indians in America. To encourage recruitment, the Highland soldiers were allowed to wear their national dress, the kilt, and carry Highland sidearms. These included the horn-carved dirk and powder horn. All other arms were banned at home in Scotland, as were the bagpipes, which the English considered, obscurely, to be some kind of weapon.

One Highlander who possessed three highly ornamented powder horns and campaigned with

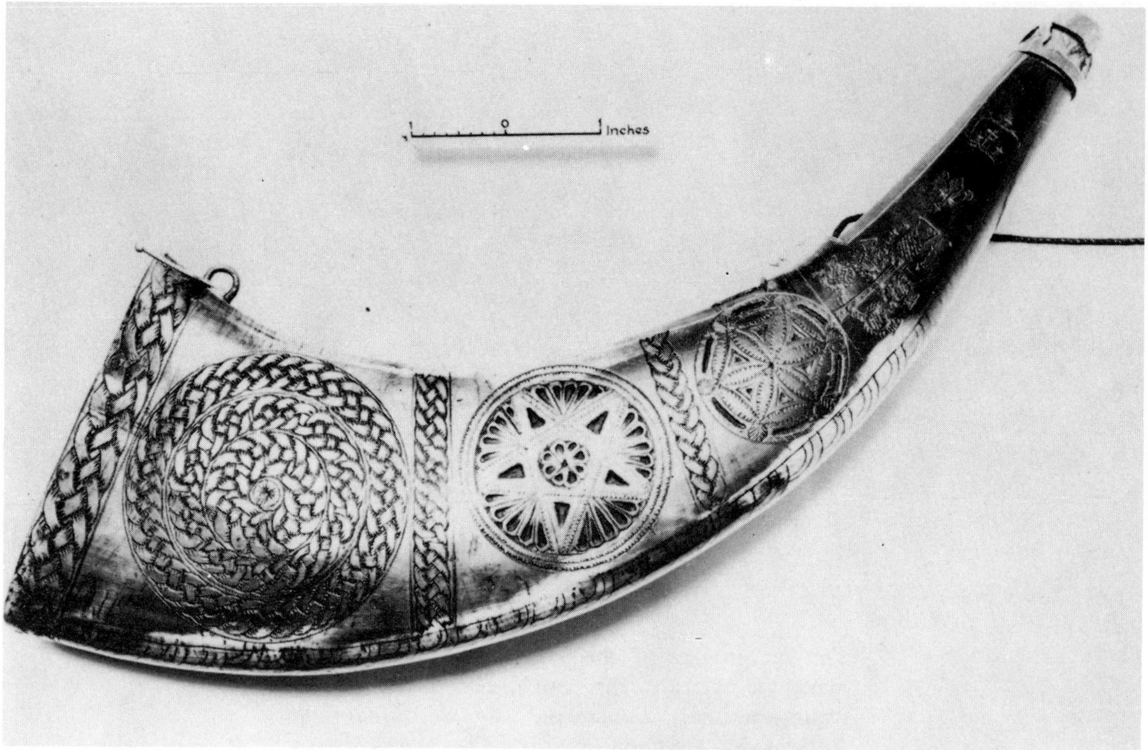

Celtic revival powder horn dated 1690. The legend inscribed on the horn runs: "A Man His Mynd Should Never Sett/ Upon The Thing Hee Cane Nott Gett." *Courtesy National Museum of Antiquities, Scotland.*

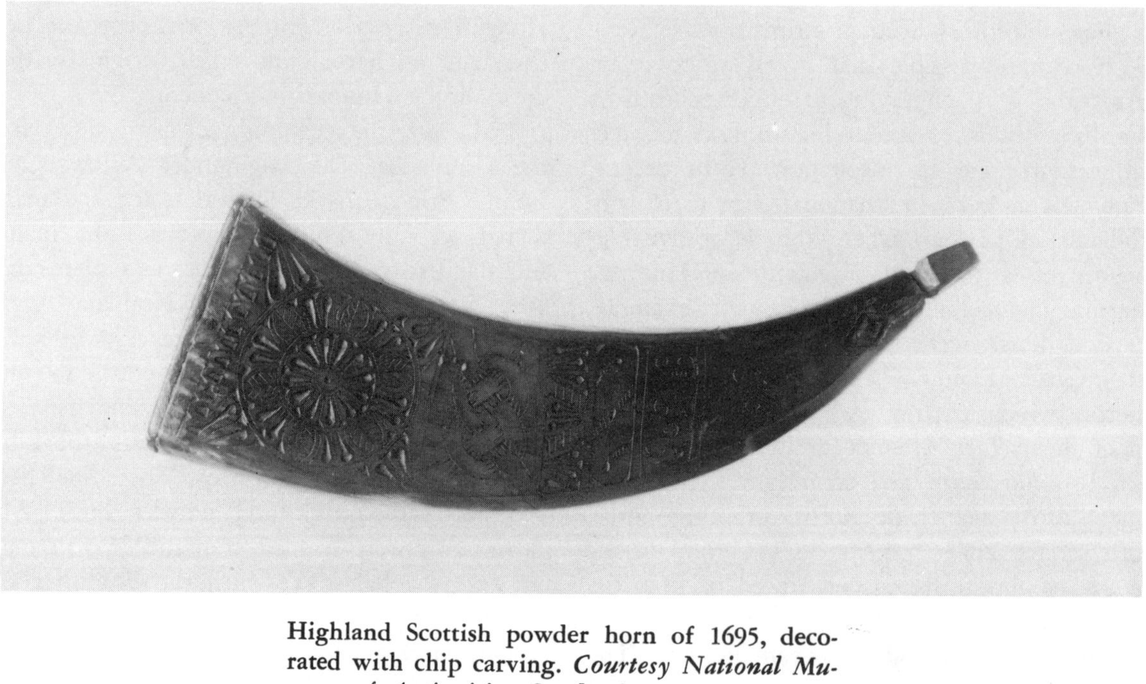

Highland Scottish powder horn of 1695, decorated with chip carving. *Courtesy National Museum of Antiquities, Scotland.*

them in America was Archibald Montgomerie, afterwards Eleventh Earl of Eglinton. He served during the French and Indian wars, and his powder horns are engraved with the Royal Arms, his own personal coat of arms, and the river routes along the Hudson and Mohawk to Lake Champlain and Ontario. Two of these horns are dated 1760.

By the time the American powder horn was fully developed as an art form in its own right, it had inherited, besides what it had derived from seventeenth-century England, many of the ornamental ideas of Scottish horn-work. These included ships, coats of arms, flags, birds of paradise, flowers, and the familiar olive branch. All these devices were in turn to be reproduced on whaling scrimshaw.

In a way it is difficult to concentrate on the ornamentation of American powder horns because of the compelling nature of their associations. There is not one of those which we still have which, if it could speak, could not tell a story of heroism just as stirring, but more true, than the horn of Count Roland. Just occasionally a horn engraver does recount his exploits, such as the artist who tells us how he fought for seven hours against the French at Ticonderoga, though he was out on the open ground and they were in a trench. Other horns bear diaries, or record wanderings to Ohio and other places, which are sometimes pictured as well as recorded in inscriptions. Other legends written on horns include proverbs, such as the one attributed to Oliver Cromwell (which stands at the head of this chapter), rhymes, place names, and dates.

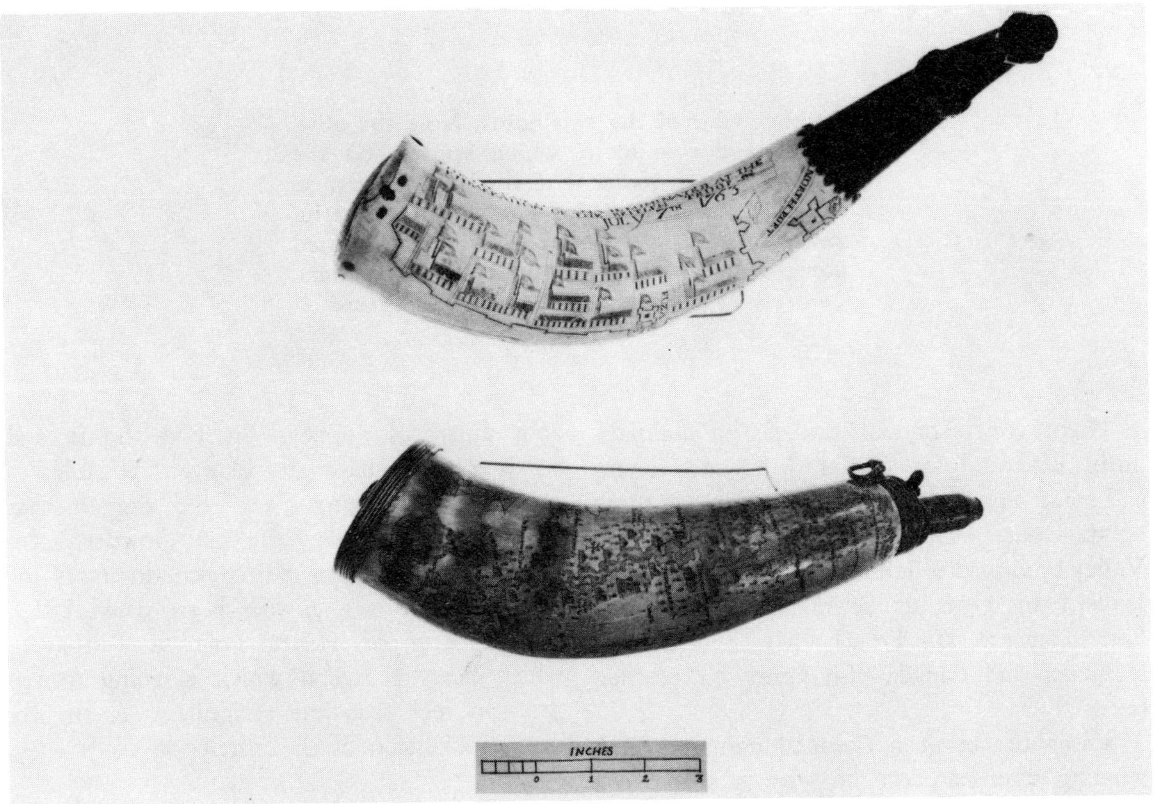

Two powder horns. The top one, dated 1767, commemorates the capture of Havana. The bottom one, dated 1770, carries a map showing the location of forts along the Mohawk River. Though labeled as English, there seems no reason to suppose that they are not Colonial American. ***Courtesy Tower of London, London, England.***

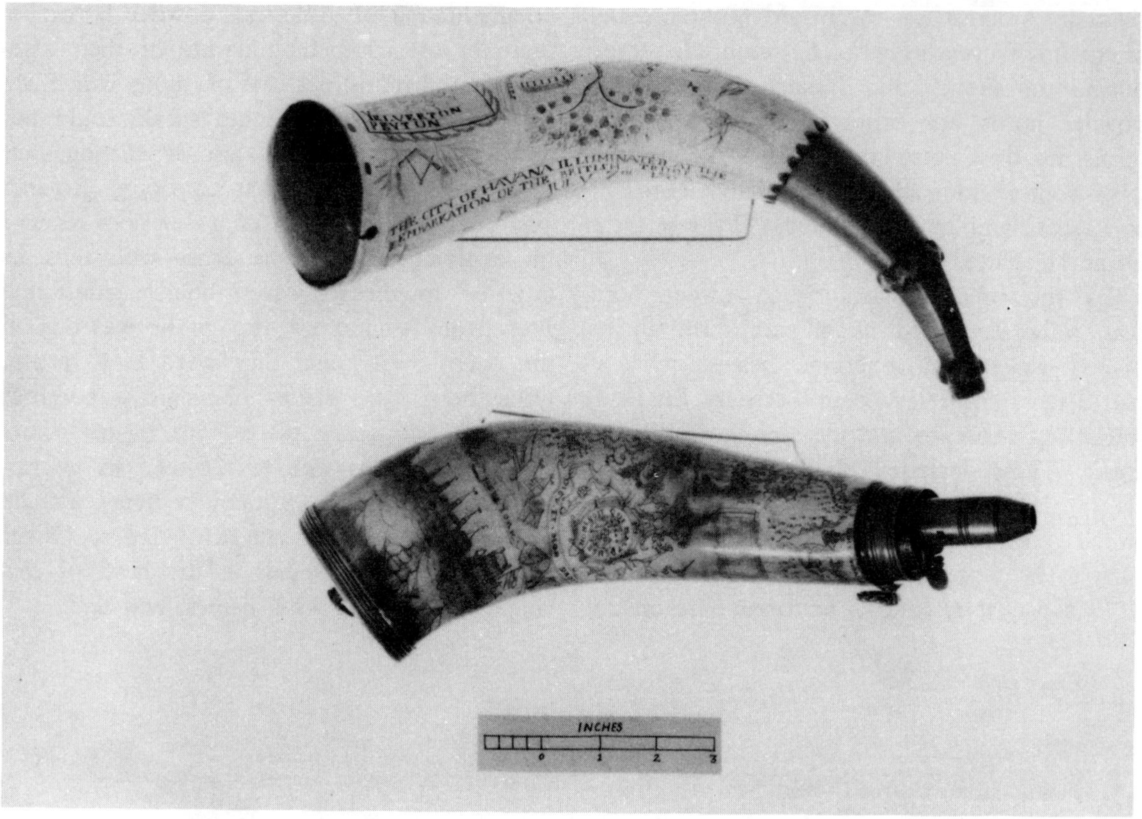

Another view of the two horns. Note the olive branch and rose motif which appears on the Havana horn, together with the bird of paradise design. Decoration of this sort will reappear on much American scrimshaw, of which ornamented horns of this sort may well be the forerunners.
Courtesy Tower of London, London, England

There are plenty of pictures of animals, birds, land and sea battles, forts and towns, and some wonderful maps, which include those of the route made through the Cumberland Valley by Brigadier John Forbes (another Highlander) in 1758, as he marched to capture Fort Duquesne. The French forts along the Alleghanies and Canada also figure on powder horns.

Strong ties between Colonial hornwork and whaling scrimshaw can be seen in shared ornaments, such as the double line and herringbone borders on some horns, and the olive branch, which I have already mentioned, which appears on at least two of the horns in the J. H. Grenville Gilbert Collection in the Metropolitan Museum in New York, Numbers 18 and 39. Weird and wonderful birds and ships also appear on both horns and whaling scrimshaw. It is even possible to point to a bridging piece and suggest that this could have been the first powder horn, engraved at sea, to be copied in ivory or whalebone. It is a powder horn, dated 1819, the property of Henry Pole of Fairhaven, which bears a legend which is going to appear on real maritime scrimshaw. A slightly amended version of the inscription reads:

> Here's death to the living
> Long life to the killer,
> Kisses to sailors' wives
> And greasy luck to whalers.

Underneath is another line "I made 100 barrels."

Not merely the decorative motifs, but also

the techniques of the hornworker recall those of the scrimshoner. I am not speaking of the professionally engraved horns, whose yellow butternut stain, varnish, or lacquer finish, and whose meticulous lines cut with a graver betray their origin, but of those made by the folk artist. The latter have been rudely carved, probably with a jack knife, and scratched, or sometimes pricked with a needle. They have been polished with pumice and had the lines of the engraving filled with soot, black cobbler's wax, grease, gunpowder or red ink, all methods used by the scrimshaw artist.

Scrimshawed Eskimo thong straightener from Alaska.

It was one thing for politicians to sever America and Britain, on the map; it was another to try to separate their art, which in the case of scrimshaw was now very much a transatlantic medium. English soldiers continued to make powder horns in Spain very like those made by American soldiers in America, and when scrimshaw finally evolved out of this international school of horn engraving it too had very mixed American and British characteristics.

One reason for this international flavor was that whaling had never been a nationally recruited profession. A British seaman, like Frank Bullen, might find himself taking orders from a black American mate of a New Bedford whaler. American whalers had been invited to settle in Dunkirk in 1786 and instruct the French in the art of whale fishing. Ships from New England had joined British whalers to fish off West Greenland and the Davis Straits for the Greenland right whale or *balaena mysticetus.* The British whalers, by the way, had already begun to experiment with a harpoon gun, which of course required a powder horn to prime it. As British whalers penetrated into the Pacific for the first time in the late eighteenth century, the Americans followed them, abandoning the Greenland fishery. The first American whaler in the Pacific was called, appropriately for 1770, "*No Duty On Tea.*" The British "South Sea" or Pacific fishery for sperm whales continued to flourish until 1790 or thereabouts, after which American whalers many times outnumbered the Britishers. Finally, when the Americans had well nigh abandoned whaling altogether after 1865, Scottish whalers continued to sail from ports such as Aberdeen, Peterhead, Dundee and Leith, until past the middle of the twentieth century.

Meanwhile a completely new fishery had been discovered, in Australian and New Zealand waters, and whalers went out to Tasmania to exploit it.

It was a striking fact that the only part of the whale which offered good, solid, material for craftwork was the outside of the jawbone, all the rest of the whale's bones being extremely spongy and cellular, so that the blood and marrow could circulate through them, and thus prevent them cracking in the enormous

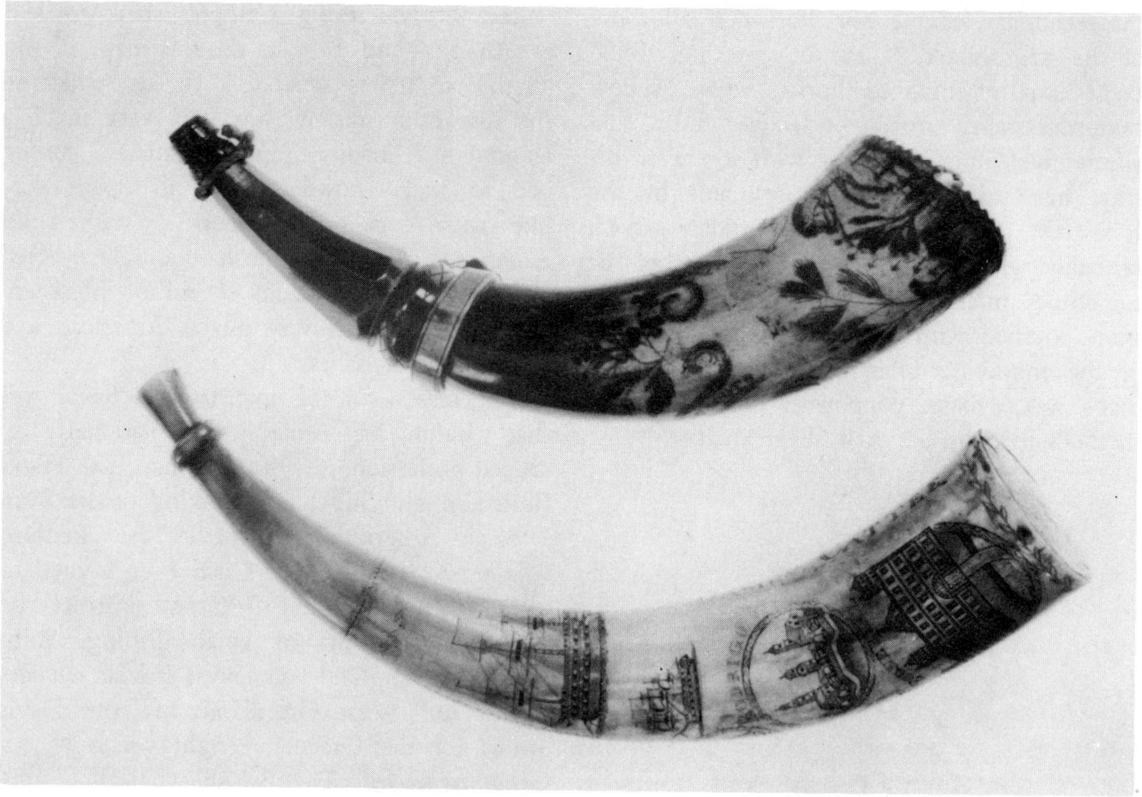

Two early nineteenth-century powder horns. The top horn is Australian, the lower English, made by James Cattee, a soldier in the Peninsular War in Spain. Both bear a strong resemblance to American scrimshaw. Notice the olive branch decoration on the lower horn. *Courtesy Tower of London, London, England.*

Australian scrimshaw. Egg cups of whalebone on a stand made of whalebone and of Huon pine from the Tasmanian forests. *Courtesy Bayly Collection, Tasmanian Museum, Hobart, Australia.*

pressures the animal had to withstand. It was the jaw, out of all the other parts of the whale, that provided the greatest interest for the whalers, because they made a point of hoisting it up and rendering it down for oil, either by boiling it or letting it drain. Both in the sperm whale and right whale fisheries the head was secured, severed from the rest of the whale, and brought aboard ship, if not too large. The head of a sperm whale was opened for the spermacetti which it contained. This was ladled out with a bucket and saved for making candles, then the jawbone was handed over to the second or third mate.

Just because the jawbone was the part of the whale designed to grapple with that monster of the deep, the giant squid, it was extremely solidly built, and it was from this jawbone, or jaw pan, that almost all bone scrimshaw was made. It would now be the responsibility of the second mate to dole out pieces of the bone to the crew who wanted to make scrimshaw, either in the shape of complete jaws, in the case of small whales, or more usually in slabs of the jaw sawn up by the ship's carpenter. Before the jaw was divided, however, it was conditioned by being towed behind the ship for a month or so until fish and birds had removed every particle of flesh.

In the Greenland fishery as well, the jaws of right whales were also saved. They were set up on deck to drain out the oil, and when they were drained, they were used to make many of the tools necessary for cutting out the baleen from the whale's mouth, such as handspikes, knives, and spades. In the Greenland fishery scrimshaw must have evolved quite naturally out of the task of preparing work tools for removing these horny ridges from the mouth of the whale.

In the sperm whale fishery, too, there were many essential tools which could usefully be made from whale jawbone, including sailmaker's rubbers, netting needles, marline spikes, and the like. Again it must have seemed an obvious idea to extend the making of tools and equipment, first to those which would be useful to a sailor's wife, and would make an acceptable homecoming present, then to more fancy items which could readily be bartered, for bottles of gin from homebound Dutch East Indiamen or tobacco from the crews of other ships spoken with in a "gam" or social exchange at sea. The range of these trade goods is astonishing, more than justifying Hermann Melville's assertion that whalers "will turn you out anything you please, in the way of a mariner's fancy." Jagging wheels, cribbage boards, trinket boxes, "swifts" for wool-winding, parasol handles, back scratchers, work boxes, studs, ink stands, cufflinks, trays, pegs, walking sticks, knife handles, baskets, knitting needles, yardsticks, bodkins, wickpickers, inlaid writing boxes, mirror boxes, earrings, collar buttons, picture frames; nothing came amiss to the versatile scrimshoner.

There was something mechanical and repetitive about all these products, however, and the scrimshaw artist only gave of his best when he was carving a personalized piece, such as a stay busk for presentation to his sweetheart. One of the benefits of being a sailor's girlfriend, and wearing his presents, was that you did not have to undergo the torture of wearing the much more restrictive professionally made corset of baleen. It was only during the brief interlude of the French Revolution and Napoleonic wars that women's waists escaped from this ordeal. The uncorseted figure became the fashion, with gauzy draperies damped slightly so that they would cling to a woman and show the classical purity of her outline. This must have meant good business for the doctor and the undertaker, but it was ruin to the stay-maker. Tom Paine must have felt glad that he had left his employment as a stay-maker in Woolwich to become a professional revolutionary.

Next to the stay busk, the whalebone picture was the favoured medium of the really gifted scrimshoner. This was a large plaque of whale jaw pan decorated with an engraving, either of a whaleship pursuing a whale, or some other theme which was not composed by the scrimshoner himself, but taken from the illustrations from some periodical, such as *Harper's Weekly* or *Godey's Lady's Book*. This reliance on themes borrowed from contemporary engraving recalls the American powder horn maker, some of whose motifs, such as

This piece of scrimshaw, although preserved in the Tasmanian Museum, Australia, was almost certainly made by an American whaleman, because it was not the custom of Tasmanian whalers to use sails on the whale boats. The picture is colored in black and green with red around the dying whale. *Courtesy The Crowther Collection, Tasmanian Museum, Hobart, Australia.*

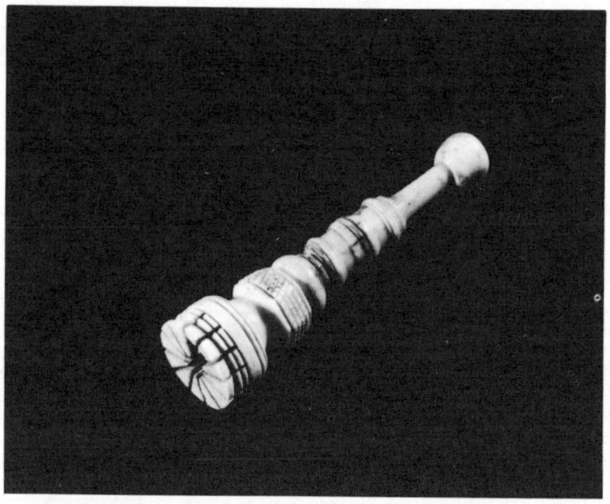

Australian scrimshaw. These are worked "head pieces," which were intended to hold parasols and were made for girl friends. *Courtesy The Crowther Collection, Tasmanian Museum, Hobart, Australia.*

the British Royal Arms, must have been copied from an engraved example, probably the head of a proclamation or something of that sort. The large whalebone pictures were supported by side brackets and top ornaments. Like the whale's teeth they were "greatly appreciated as ornaments to put over the fireplace in the kitchen or in other rooms of the house."[1] Sometimes the whalebone picture was without brackets; it was then intended to be set straight into a wooden frame. Occasionally the large pictures are given a hole at the top for suspension, and finished with a scrimshaw border round about. They are obviously intended to hang on the wall. Occasionally half jawbones, or whole jawbones would be scrimshawed with a picture, sometimes surrounded by a border. Sometimes they were supported on little pedestals scrimshawed from whalebone.

These ornaments would be treasured by the family of the scrimshoner and proudly shown to visitors because they were made in the days when idleness was still considered a vice, and not the natural ambition of everyone. I was brought up in a small Scottish fishing town, and played with the children of many seamen, lighthouse keepers, and coastguards. Looking back on those far off days I recall that the best room was always filled with objects which the man of the house had made while away at sea.

Not just whalebone, but bones of other marine creatures as well were employed by the scrimshoner. Frank Bullen, a British seaman, whom stark hunger compelled to ship for "that horror, a cruise on a whaler" recalls that: "I once caught a shark nine feet long. It was my intention to prepare that useless and unornamental article so dear to sailors, a walking stick made of a shark's backbone."[2]

The favored material was whale jawbone, however, partly because there was so much of it to spare; the jaw of just one sperm whale, measuring eighteen feet long, would be sufficient to set all the scrimshoners in the crew to work, partly because it offered such an attractive material, rich, creamy and dense, with agreeable black fleckings.

Frank Bullen describes how a whale was captured by his ship, the *Cachalot,* and adds: "The lower jaw of this whale measured exactly nineteen feet in length from the opening of the mouth, or say the last of the teeth, to the point. For the time it was hauled aft out of the way, and secured to the lash rail. After every sign of the operations (removing the spermacetti from the head) had been cleared away the jaw was brought out. The great jaw pans were sawn off, and placed at the disposal of anybody who wanted pieces of bone for 'scrimshaw' or carved work. This is a very favorite pastime on board whalers, though in ships such as ours, the crew have little opportunity for doing anything, hardly any leisure during daylight being allowed. But our carpenter was a famous workman at 'scrimshaw,' and he started half a dozen walking sticks forthwith. A favorite design is to carve the bone into the similitude of a rope, with 'worming' of smaller line along its lays. A handle is carved out of a whale's tooth, and insets of baleen, silver, cocoa tree, or ebony, give variety and finish. The tools used are of the roughest. Some old files, softened in the fire, and filed into grooves something like saw teeth, are most used—but old knives, sail needles, and chisels are pressed into service. The work turned out would, in many cases, take a very high place in an exhibition of turnery, though never a lathe was near it. Of course a long time is taken over it, especially the polishing, which is done with oil and whiting, if it can be got—powdered pumice if it cannot."[3]

The files which have had their temper drawn by the fire, and then had their faces refiled into steps, before being re-tempered, are basic tools of the bone and ivory carver. They were used by the craftsmen of Dieppe in their ivory-carving workshops, under the name of *grêles.* You can still walk into an ivory-carving workshop in Central Africa, such as

1. W. Bryden, *Scrimshaw* (Tasmanian Museum and Art Gallery, Hobart, Australia, 1963).

2. Frank Hullen, *The Cruise of the Cachalot* (London: Smith Elder & Co., 1911), pp. 22–24.

3. Ibid., pp. 81–83.

the workroom of Jackson Sadiq in Blantyre, Malawi, and find the work bench littered with exactly the same kind of tools, made in exactly the same way as those used aboard the *Cachalot.* One can only speculate about how tools of this sort got as far afield as Malawi, but their presence aboard an American whaleship may well be a relic of the settlement of some American whalemen at Dunkirk in 1786 who may have visited Dieppe, or else tools like these may have been taken aboard whalers by Dieppe carvers fleeing from empressment in the French navy.

Not every scrimshoner was as well equipped as the carpenter of the *Cachalot.* "Throughout the Pacific," says Hermann Melville, "and also in Nantucket, and New Bedford, and Sag Harbour, you will come across lively sketches of whales and whaling scenes, graven by the fishermen themselves, on . . . ladies' busks wrought out of the right whale bone, and other like skrimshander articles, as the whalemen call the numerous little ingenious contrivances they elaborately carve out of the rough material, in their hours of ocean leisure. Some of them have little boxes of dentistical looking implements, specially intended for the skrimshandering business. But in general, they toil with their jack-knives alone; and with that almost omnipotent tool of the sailor, they will turn you out anything you please."[4]

A very wide variety of tools was used to do the actual engraving of whalebone, as opposed to the carving. They included specialist tools made by the whaler's blacksmith or carpenter from old saw blades: sail needles, called "pickwicks," which might be set in a wooden or bone handle, cut-down cabin knives, and sharpened nails set in stumps of wood, identical with those used by the Eskimos for making scrimshaw.

If a scrimshoner was engraving an original design he would probably draw it directly onto the surface of the whalebone, but if he were using an illustration, he would trace it, and paste the tracing onto the whalebone, or perhaps paste the illustration itself. Then he might prick through every line of the picture with a needle, rub the paper off, and join up the pricks.

The designs of scrimshaw are of particular importance in that, unless a piece is dated, it is usually only the design which is likely to yield any clue as to when and where it was made. Sometimes the clues given by a design are fairly obvious ones. Thus a scrimshawed picture of whale boats under sail is certainly American, because it was not the custom of Tasmanian whalers to use sails in the actual whale boats. Other indications are less definite. A whaler which is a barque, brig, or schooner, is much more likely to be Australian than American, because there were only three full-rigged ships whaling out of Hobart Town; they were the *Pacific,* the *Jane,* and the *Offley.*

If it is difficult to identify the ships which sail across scrimshaw by the cut of their jib, it is much easier to make a guess at the date of that other recurrent theme of the scrimshoner, the ladies. I say ladies deliberately because scrimshoners did not love to portray the humble daughters of the poor, but rather belles of rank and fashion. As womens' fashions changed much more frequently than the fashion in ships it will eventually be possible to marry up every piece of scrimshaw to its date and say "the subject of this picture is wearing a crinoline, so it could not have been made before 1850."

Great ingenuity was shown by the scrimshoner in putting to use the materials which he found ready to his hand to aid him in his task. The sharks which were frequently caught and hauled on board, to prevent them eating up too much of the fast whale, would be skinned and the sharkskin dried and used instead of sandpaper to polish whalebone. Soot from the chimneys of the try works and the galley was also collected and used as a pigment. Gunpowder and black tobacco juice were utilized for the same purpose, sometimes mixed with oil, verdigris green was scraped off the copper kettles of the ship, black, blue and red ink obtained from the captain's steward. The blubber scraps fed into the furnace of the try works left a fine ash which was slightly caustic. This made an ideal polish, as

4. Herman Melville, *Moby Dick* (London: Dent, Everyman Edition, 1968), p. 237.

This Australian scrimshawed mantelpiece ornament was made by scratching in a design transferred from a popular magazine and then wiping in the color with a thumb. ***Courtesy The Crowther Collection, Tasmanian Museum, Hobart, Australia.***

it partly ate away the surface of the whalebone, just as oxalic acid does the surface of a marble statue when it is used to polish it. Damp wood ash from the galley, sail maker's wax, powdered pumice, whiting, china clay, and whale oil were also used as polishes.

Very little has been written about the patrons of scrimshaw, but patrons were important. As Hermann Melville says, getting paid for something we have done is one of the things which reconcile us to the many ills of life. The thought of what he would receive for a finished piece must have encouraged many a scrimshoner to persevere with his long task. Pieces of scrimshaw found their way into the hands of specialist dealers in natural curiosities. The shop of one of these dealers has been well described by the famous Victorian naturalist, Frank Buckland, in 1857.[5] "Those who have visited the French seaport of Havre de Grace must well recollect the innumerable curiosity shops which therein abound; curiosity shops, not like those in the Wardour or the Dean Streets of London, where are exposed for ignominious sale the cast off Penates (household goods) of London folk, both rich and poor; but real curiosity shops, on whose shelves are arranged in a strange medley the products, animal, vegetable, and mineral, of far distant and little known climes, brought home by the sailors who navigate the numerous and busy trading ships which line the quays, and

5. Frank Buckland, *Curiosities of Natural History,* First Series, Fifth Edition (London: William Clowes and Sons Ltd., 1960), p. 291.

Australian scrimshaw in whale jawpan. The legend beneath this hanging scrimshaw picture reads: "The *Pacific* whaling ship Captain Robert Gardiner of Hobart Town homeward bound, 900 barrels, sperm oil, 10 months out 1848." Only two other Australian whalers out of Hobart Town were full-rigged ships, the *Jane* and the *Offley*. The rest were barques, brigs or schooners. *Courtesy The Crowther Collection, Tasmanian Museum, Hobart, Australia.*

we may almost say the streets of this French Liverpool. Let us enter one of these shops and examine its contents. On the one shelf we see curiously carved baskets, cut with ingenuity from a cocoa-nut brought from the South Sea Islands, and beside it armlets of the same all useful nut, from the Storrs and Mortimers (Victorian shopkeepers) of the islands aforesaid.

"On the neighbouring shelf are displayed the products of the Arctic regions, snow spectacles used by the Esquimaux in his journeys over the frozen snows of his ice-bound but well-beloved home, bartered most likely to the mate of yon tall-masted whaling ship for a drink of brandy from his flask, or a sixpenny Birmingham knife. Teeth of that monster of the deep, the cachelot whale, lie there, mixed with the whalebone from the capacious mouth, or, as we may justly call it, infusorial trap of the true, or right whale; the oil from whose sides fills those greasy looking barrels just hoisted out of the hold of the floating oil-shop close by.

"On the longest 'fin' of this whalebone, behold a rude but correct portrait, carved with a sailor's jack-knife, of the oak and iron bound vessel whose comfortable berths formed the only home of the artist when daring the perils of the Northern Ocean."

It is not difficult to see why scrimshaw has become the most sought after and admired of all forms of folk art. The very qualities which were necessary to enable an American whaleman to construct a piece of scrimshaw have helped to perpetuate his name as the greatest of all self-taught artists. Scrimshaw is painstaking; it has not been dashed off in five minutes, but taken weeks or months of the most laborious toil, undertaken with the rudest possible tools. People realize that if a work of art means so much to an artist that he must go on doing it, even under conditions of the greatest difficulty, such as those which pertained on a whaleship, it must be genuine. The artist must believe in himself, and this belief in himself transfers itself to the admirer of his work. Just as the public, in the long run, are always more ready to prefer genuine and honest craftsmanship to something made by an artist with his tongue in his cheek, so the subjects of scrimshaw have helped to commend it to art lovers all over the world. Here are themes which the ordinary person in the street can both understand and appreciate: the way of a ship on the sea, women, portrayed not as playthings but as ideal beings, and conflicts, against apparently hopeless odds, bravely undertaken. The short lives and tragic ends of many of the scrimshoners cannot fail to shed a luster onto their works and make us interested in them, just as that prosaic citizen of Northampton, New Jersey, Quaker John Woolman, seems to have remained unaffected by art until the night when in 1763, he pitched his tent by the banks of the Great Lehie, the western branch of the Delaware, near Fort Allen. "Near our Tent," he records in his Journal, "on the Sides of large Trees peeled for that Purpose, were various Representations of Men going to, and returning from the Wars, and of some killed in Battle; this being a Path heretofore used by Warriours."[6]

The Pacific and Atlantic too were a path heretofore used by warriors. "These bones," wrote an American whaleman "Are their only memorial."

6. John Woolman, *The Journal of John Woolman* (London: Dent, Everyman's Edition, 1944), p. 106.

3

THE AGE OF BONE AND HORN

Stone Age Carving

IN the eighteen forties the artistic and scientific world was astounded by the discovery, made by an amateur archaeologist called Brouillet, of a bone engraving of two hinds in a cave at Chaffaud, near Savigné, in France. After a period of shock, while the learned world digested this find, it gradually dawned on everyone that a new kind of art had been discovered, completly different from that of any other civilization, and that the caves and grottos of France, hitherto regarded as being important for penning goats and ripening cheeses, were the art galleries and museums in which would be displayed to a wondering public the longest-lasting and the most widely distributed era of art in the history of mankind.

The art of the New Stone Age begins when the furthest extended fingers of the glaciers which were strangling Europe began to melt and recede, shortly after 40,000 B.C. It runs down to the second millenium B.C., where it disappears in the Arctic art of Scandinavia and Russia, or possibly simply moves further north to become incorporated in polar art. The vast time scale of this school of art is matched by an equally vast geographical stage, which stretches from the Norwegian Arctic to the southernmost tips of Spain and Sicily, and from the extreme west of Spain to the plains of Russia. Even these confines are merely those which scholarly convention has decided to impose upon it, because paintings, very similar to those made by the artists of the Stone Age, begin in North Africa and continue down to the Cape. As this African art is mostly confined to painting, not bone carving, we can conveniently forget about it.

The long history of Stone Age art is split up into well-defined periods: the Aurignacian, Solutrian, Azilian and Tardenoisian, styles which succeed one another at intervals of several thousand years. Running side by side with them, not quite merged with them, are Spanish Levant Art, which is closely related to the art of Africa, and Arctic Art. It is strange to reflect at a time when artists are always being told by non-artists that they must be contemporary and try to find new styles for themselves, rather than copy the old ones, that Stone Age artists who are among the finest in the world were apparently content to go on in the old ways, carving in the traditional manner for thousands of years. If interviewed on this topic outside his cave, a Stone Age artist would probably have pointed out that great art is not born in a day; he was trying to surpass the best efforts of his grandfather, who in turn had tried to outdo the efforts of previous generations.

Though Stone Age art was by no means confined to bone carving, it struck the dominant note. Bone served as a sketchbook for the cave painters and sculptors; the head of a hind, engraved on a shoulder blade of the same animal, has been faithfully reproduced in paint on the wall of a cave at Santander in Spain. Bone and horn possessed several other advantages as the chosen medium for the best artists. It was the substance most often handled by the cave men, who made from it all their hunting and domestic equipment. Long familiarity in handling it had given them mastery in the art of carving the material. Essential items made from bone included harpoons and spear heads, spear throwers, arrow straighteners, daggers, needle cases, forks, spoons, clasps, whistles and the like.

Jewelry, which may seem to us an ornament, probably had amuletic power to the men and women of the Stone Age. The small carvings of women with exaggerated sexual characteristics and of game animals for which the period is so famous are almost certainly amulets or fetishes, carried about to be invoked for success in procreation or the hunt. Sculptures in clay or stone were usually too bulky to be carried around, and an artist might hesitate before entrusting his best sculptures to the wall of a cave, where they would be irretrievably fixed, and where he might never see them again, for the Stone Age men were essentially hunters, and were always moving around in search of game.

Horn and bone had already assumed their importance as substances charged with magical significance. Human bones and skulls are still worshipped in Naples, in Italy, and bone has always been a material preferred for purposes of divination and sorcery, as in the case of the oracle bones of ancient China. Horns have always been a fertility symbol, possibly because of their phallic shape. On a stone bas-relief in a cave at Laussel a very plump nude woman holds a buffalo horn. Bones were also charged with messages of spiritual importance addressed to the gods. At Vestonice, in South Moravia in Czechoslovakia, the body of a young woman was found, buried with her legs and arms tied, either because she was a human sacrifice, or for fear she might rise from her unquiet grave and trouble the living. Covering her was a layer of red ochre, which to Stone Age folk symbolized the vital force, and two mammoth shoulder blades, one of which was covered with a mysterious inscription.

The very facility which Stone Age sculptors acquired in working bone and horn must have encouraged them to do their best work in it. The floors of the caves in which they lived are littered with thousands of bone tools. Even allowing for the long period over which these homes were occupied, it must still have been possible, for Stone Age carvers, to work this intractable material fairly quickly. It is, then, not surprising that many of the masterpieces of the era are made from bone and horn, particularly during periods, such as the Magdalenian, when reindeer horn was the chosen material for most sculptors.

It is difficult to appreciate Stone Age art without some understanding of the world in which the artists lived, because their art reflects its surroundings very closely. Some unexplained phenomenon, such as a deviation of the normal alignment of the Polar axis, or an upsurge of solar radiation, had dropped the temperature in Europe to a level where rivers froze in the winter, and a harsh, cold climate prevailed even in summer. The continent became a suitable grazing ground for the most cold-loving animals, such as the mammoth, the wooly rhinoceros, and the reindeer. A mantle of ice covered Europe from Northern France to the top of Norway; further south, great glaciers sheathed the Alps, and stood out as advanced posts of the frozen north on the *massif central* of France and the high sierras of Spain. The icy breath of the glaciers blasted all save a low and stunted vegetation of heather, reindeer moss, lichens, and dwarf trees, such as tiny azaleas, willows, and birches. The brief summer saw a riot of gaily colored flowers appear in the patches of grass which appeared among the melting snow. Browsing among the violets, poppies and saxifrages, chewing the cotton grass, heather and reindeer moss which flourished between the gaps in the glaciers, moved the mammoth and woolly-haired rhinoceros, the buffalo, the musk ox, the saiga antelope, the ibex, the steppe horse, the steppe ass, the roe deer, elk, and wild sheep. Savage predators hung on the skirts of the great herds: the cave lion, the cave panther, the cave hyena, the lynx, the brown bear, and the wolf.

Between all these animals and the Stone Age artist there existed the same relationship which was later to exist between the American scrimshoner and the whale. The artist learned to portray his quarry while hunting it. He had to kill to eat, for there were few fruits and berries to be gathered and agriculture had not yet begun. What was more, the hunter believed that the more skillful a carver or engraver he was, the greater would be his success in the chase. The figures of the animals which he engraved on his weapons were intended to invoke a magic influence on them when he directed the weapons against his prey. Some faint recollection of this idea still prevailed in whaling days in the nineteenth century, when on the first of May, British whalers sent up to the masthead of their ship a garland, made from ribbands contributed by their sweethearts, containing a model of the whaleship in which they sailed.

The Stone Age hunters tackled game in various ways, which they faithfully recorded for us on their bone engravings. They singled out young mammoths from the main herd, surrounded them, and speared them. They dug pit traps for adult mammoths, and camouflaged them with a brushwood covering, containing a sharpened stake on which the great beast would impale itself once it had fallen into the pit. Buffalo were culled out of the herd and driven into swamps or defiles with no outlet. Wild horses were stampeded over cliffs. At Solutré, near Lyons, France there is a cliff at the foot of which has been found an eight-foot thick layer of bones, estimated to contain the remains of 100,000 wild horses. The cave bear and cave lion, the most formidable enemies of the Stone Age hunter, were disposed of by a bombardment of heavy boulders from above as they issued from the mouth of their cave.

The slaughter of so many animals produced a wealth of raw material for the artist. Sometimes this was carefully sorted out, as at the stations of the mammoth hunters of Moravia, in Czechoslovakia, where waste bones were thrown into pits specially dug for rubbish, while selected pieces of bone were carefully put to one side and arranged neatly so as to be ready for use. One studio, at Predmosti, contained thirteen wolf skulls, fifty mammoth teeth, and thirteen mammoth tusks. Not all sculptors were (or are) as tidy as this. On many Stone Age sites bones, partly burned and split to get at the marrow, littered the floor in a thick layer.

Unlike the cave painters, who had to work by artificial light as they painted magical pictures on the walls of the innermost recesses of the caves to ensure good hunting, the Stone Age sculptors seem to have preferred to work outside, hard by the hearth fire which burned continually in the vestibule of the cave, which was at the same time a home, fortress, and temple.

A few simple tools enabled the sculptor to carry out his wonderful carvings: a knife, probably formed from small sharp flint blades, set in a wooden handle, a flint saw with notched edges, wooden or bone wedges for dividing larger blocks of bone, abrasive blocks of sandstone, for shaping and polishing bone carvings, and a flint drill, probably held in some kind of wooden handle. The most useful tools at the disposal of the carver were flint scrapers. These would scrape off a feathery shaving of bone, and, by removing a tiny fraction of the material at a time, enable the sculptor to retain complete control of the carving as he shaped it. The flint scraper could be instantly trimmed so as to scoop out any shape of hollow which the artist wanted. Some of them which have survived are made in shapes rather like the modern-day scorper which a sculptor uses, with two round ends and a narrow waist. Engraving was carried out by means of pointed flakes of flint which served as burins.

Carvings made by the sculptors included those of the human figure, such as one on a small bone wand, possiby a piece of magical equipment, which is also carved with bold

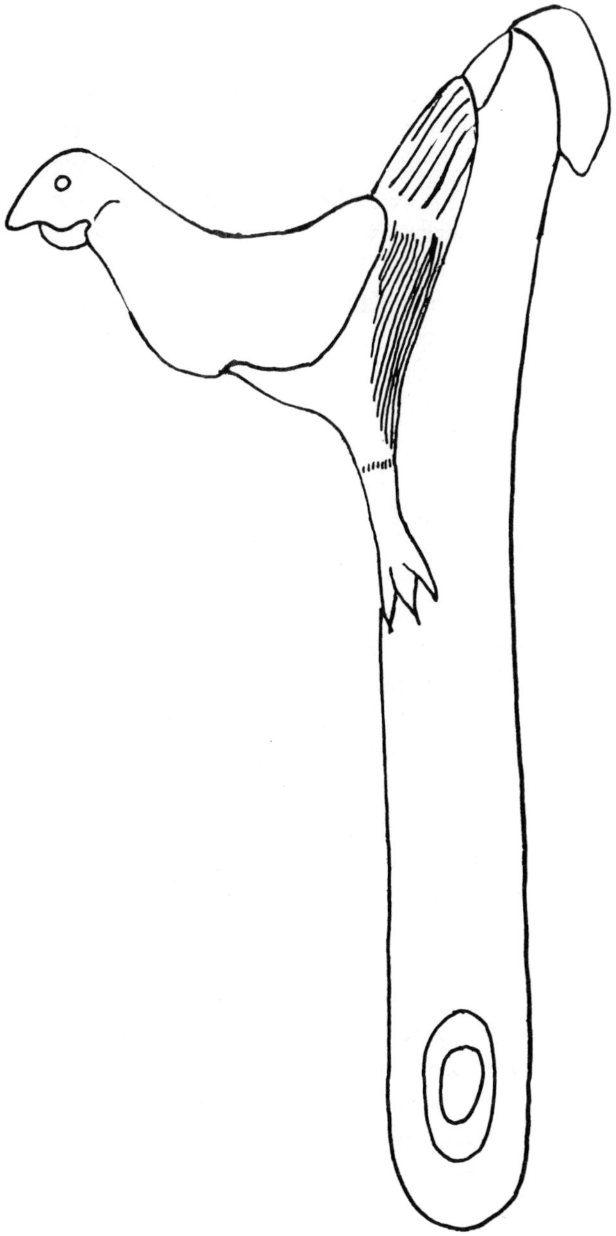

Black cock carved on a spear, from the cave of Mas d' Azil, France.

Buffalo carved in reindeer antler, from the cave of La Madeleine, France.

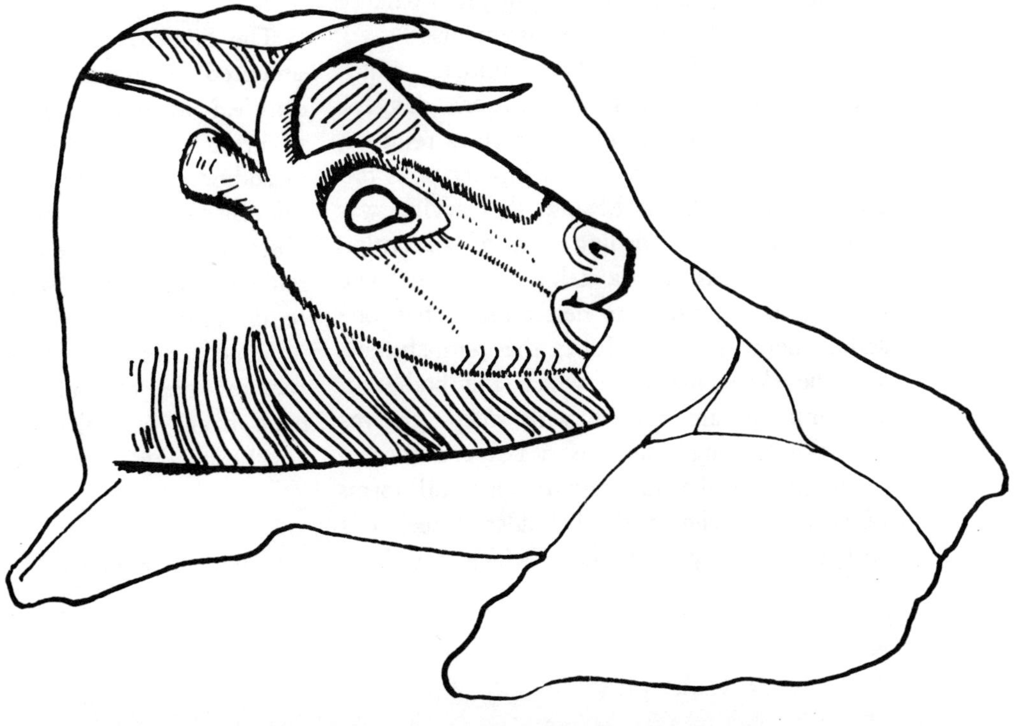

abstract shapes. It comes from Ahrensburgh in West Germany. However, human figures were always less favored than those of animals. These include magnificent sculptures such as the head of a neighing horse, carved in reindeer antler, from Mas d'Asil, and the buffalo turning its head (see line drawing) from La Madeleine, both in France. Although these sculptures probably had their useful side, in that they were magical fetishes, the carver was at his best when wedding sculptures to practical objects, such as spear throwers. Not for him Ruskin's dictum that nothing that was useful could also be beautiful! He took the greatest pains to adapt his carving to the needs of the tool or weapon which he was decorating. A dagger would have a good, solid, bulging handle, which could be gripped easily. A spear thrower, which enabled the hunter to throw his spear for a greater distance than he could with the unaided hand, needed to have a hook at the end so as to hold the butt end of the spear. The carver always sculpted the animals which ended the spear thrower, so as to allow for just such a hook, even though it was sometimes a little difficult to do so. If he carved a mammoth as a finial, it would have a short, stubby tail cocked up in the air. If he made a chamois, two birds would perch on its rump. Sometimes the legs of the animals, instead of being just indicated in the flat, would be carved freestanding, probably so as to cut away enough of the material to reduce the weight of the spear thrower slightly and balance it exactly to the hunter's requirements.

The shape of the various animals which decorate the ends of spear throwers, daggers, or arrow straighteners, animals such as reindeer, mammoth, ibex, chamois, and blackcock, is often triangular. This is because the carving was made from the branching part of an antler, where it widens into a delta shape. In these carvings it is possible to detect more than one style; there is the realistic, the semi-abstract, and the skeletonized, in which the bodies of the animals are carved with deep grooves cut with a gouge, such as a beaver's tooth.

In spite of the admiration which all forms of cave art excite in the beholder, I feel it is still true to say that those which are most prized are the engravings. "Scrimshaw," would be a better term to describe these pieces, rather than "engraving," because they have many points of resemblance to the scrimshaw made by American whalemen in the nineteenth century. Hermann Melville pointed out that "Long exile from Christendom and civilisation inevitably restores a man to . . . what is called savagery . . . now one of the peculiar characteristics of the savage in his domestic hours is his wonderful patience of industry."[1] Stone Age designs are incised on bone or ivory and then filled in with pigment, such as charcoal or iron oxide, mixed with animal fat or vegetable oil as a binder. Usually none of this pigment has survived burial in the earth, though there is a stag, engraved on an arrow straightener from Castille in Spain, which has been lined in red ochre. Some lines are deeply scored and cross-hatched, and show similarities to Eskimo scrimshaw as well as that carried out by whalemen.

The patterns for scrimshaw vary from rough drawings intended to be elaborated in a painting on the cave wall, to elaborate meander patterns, stylized human figures, mythological beings, and above all, animals, birds, and fish. Mammoth, reindeer, horses, swans, and bison, along with many other creatures, occur on these engravings. Occasionally the legs of an animal have been drawn in several different positions, or it has been scrimshawed again and again on the same piece of reindeer antler, showing a restless hunt for perfection.

The Stone Age carvers soon became so enamoured of scrimshaw that they no longer confined its use to magical pictures intended to bring good luck in hunting. They used it, in addition, for pure ornament, decorating useful objects, such as spoons and forks, with an abstract design, a double line filled in the middle with cross strokes, in a way very reminiscent of Eskimo designs.

Some scrimshaw consists of neither realistic pictures nor ornamental abstract designs. A bone from the Pekarna cave near Mokra, in Czechoslovakia, is covered with rows of notches,

1. Herman Melville, p. 237.

cut in irregular rows and pointing in different directions. Obviously this is some kind of written message, possibly the tally of game killed on a hunt. Later on we shall see how the Chinese were helped by scrimshaw to finalize their ideas of writing and adopt a definitive script.

Scrimshaw came to the aid of the sculptor as well as the engraver. A statue of a cave lion would have arrows scrimshawed, not carved, on its flanks, to show that it had been wounded. The hair of animals was minutely portrayed by the same means. A horse would have engraved on it not merely the hairs of its mane, but the pattern of ridges over its whole coat. Sometimes abstract patterns will be scrimshawed, or even deeply scored, on sculptures in the round, even though these patterns need have no connection with the object which has been carved. I feel this kind of decoration has no purpose to it, save sheer ornamentation, but if these grooves and cuts show any resemblance, or apparent resemblance, to the bony structure of the animal portrayed, they will be hailed as "skeletonised" or "x-ray" patterns.

Were the lessons of Stone Age art transmitted to any successors? Faint echoes of the art of the caves seem to reach us as we look at a collection of Eskimo bone carvings. There is the same predominance of animal over human figures, the same avoidance of landscape and narrative art. The resemblances between the scrimshaw carried out by both sets of artists has already been mentioned. Decorative devices are often similar, such as the double line, broken with lines of ticks, which is a great standby of Eskimo art and which ornaments Stone Age forks. Deeply scored parallel lines decorate Eskimo animal figures; they are also to be found on the stylized female figurines from Dolni Vestonice in Czechoslovakia. Even the dotted line, probably the most often used Eskimo device, occurs on a spatula-shaped object from the Pekarna Cave near Mokra in Czechoslovakia.

It seems difficult not to assume that at least some of the Stone Age hunters (such as Chancelade Man, who was very Eskimo-like in appearance) wandered north in pursuit of the mammoths, as they followed the melting glaciers towards the Pole, and were absorbed into the civilization of the Arctic. Connected with this civilization is the art of other northern people besides the Eskimo, including the Lapps, whose very attractive scrimshaw recalls that of the Stone Age artists and the Eskimo alike. So it is possible to think of the art of the Stone Age as something not lost and gone forever, but merely the opening chapter of the continuous practice of man's oldest craft.

4

GRAPES AND GODDESSES

Carving in the Near East

THE story of bone carving in the near East is an obscure one, in which conjecture must play a much larger part than demonstration. It is, however, possible to postulate that the inspiration for Near Eastern carving comes ultimately from the carved bone plaques made by the Scythians. By the second century before Christ, the Scythian animal carving tradition had been transmitted to Parthia. Like the Scythians, the Parthians lived on the very edge of the Roman Empire; both peoples had partly merged their traditional arts in the new styles of decoration acquired from Greek and Roman traders, styles which had percolated through the Roman Empire to its furthest borders.

In Parthia, bone carving developed into a high art. Bone figurines were manufactured by the funerary craftsmen, whose workshops lined the approaches to the cemeteries. At their booths, relatives of the dead, and mourners, would buy small representations of protective deities, which were placed with the dead man in his tomb. Popular protective figures included a cavalryman (more will be said about the Parthian horse in a moment) and an unknown, naked goddess. As in all religious art, there were gradations of style and degrees of finish, and the prices were adjusted accordingly, so that even the poorest could buy something. The goddess might be a delightfully abstract carving who looked like a clothes peg. She would be cut from a single hollow animal bone, and her features indicated with crude vigor, the circles of the eyes being scribed in with a pair of metal compasses, the lines of her body cut in with a file, and her legs indicated by a simple bifurcation made with a saw. If you were prepared to pay more, you could have a much more elaborate figure, in which the goddess was carved out in silhouette, in an outline figure not very different from that of contemporary Parthian mother-of-pearl silhouette pieces for inlay in furniture. The best figures were little masterpieces in their own right. In spite of the fact that they had to have jointed arms, they managed to convey all the allure of the Parthian belle, with her high piled coiffure, or elaborate turban, her wasp waist, pinched in just below deep breasts, and her broad hips cut across by a narrow girdle.

More ambitious in their treatment, though less effective from the aesthetic point of view, are a series of bone plaques, made in Parthia, but found in Olbia in South Russia, which were once part of the decoration of a piece of furniture. They depict a banquet scene, in which a king feasts amidst an entertainment staged by nude dancers and tumblers.

One of the factors which may have pushed Parthian craftsmen to excel in bone carving was the fact that they were called on to supply large quantities of minutely shaped pieces of horn for the bows carried by the Parthian light cavalry. A composite bow was a sandwich of wood, horn, glue and a thick sinew, which in later times was the thick tendon which ran down the inside of the leg of an ox. Armed with these bows, which were carefully shaped so as to impart the greatest force to an arrow, the ends curving away from the archer, the grip curving towards him, the Parthian horseman was invincible. He could ride towards the lines of an enemy army firing arrows as he approached, arrows delivered with such power that they would outrange the bows carried by Parthia's principal enemies, the Romans, and penetrate armor even if shot from some considerable distance. When the foe, maddened by the clouds of arrows fired into their midst, broke their lines and rushed out to come to grips with the elusive mounted bowmen, the Parthian cavalry simply retreated. As they fled, however, they turned round in the saddle and delivered another deadly shower of arrows, fired at their pursuers. This form of fighting retreat became proverbial among the Romans as the "Parthian shot."

Not surprisingly, the Romans disliked the Parthians so much that they did not want to have anything to do with them, or their art. This attitude is exemplified by the Roman poet Horace, who becomes very annoyed with the Parthians not merely for defeating the Romans, but for settling their prisoners of war as contented colonists on their northeastern border. Another reason why Parthian bone art found no response in Rome itself was because the materials which the Romans considered suitable for furniture had become more and more exotic, such as imported tortoiseshell and citron wood. A humble substance like bone would probably be belittled as being too ordinary and not luxurious enough.

Other parts of the Roman Empire, however, such as Egypt, were more receptive to Parthian art. Egypt had become part of the empire of Alexander the Great and had then passed into the personal possession of the Roman Emperors. The Copts, the descendants of the ancient Egyptians, had been given a very low status by their Roman masters, and were so impoverished that they could no longer employ in their art the rich materials characteristic of Egypt in the days of the Pharoahs. Instead they were forced to work in humble substances such as wood. It is not surprising, then, that they took to bone carving enthusiastically. The Copts were in touch with Parthia, and even introduced figures of Parthian cavalrymen into the central places of their tapestries; there is an example of just such a tapestry in the Louvre. They may have been introduced to Parthian bone carving by means of Parthian furniture with inlaid bone plaques imported to Egypt. Many of the early Coptic bone plaques are obviously intended for furniture, as can be seen from the holes which pierce them. Through these holes they were intended to be pegged to a wooden base.

Cupid in vine scrolls. Coptic relief carved in bone of the third or fourth century. ***Courtesy Victoria and Albert Museum, London, England.***

Coptic bone plaques from Behnessa, probably fourth century. ***Courtesy Victoria and Albert Museum, London, England.***

Another reason why the Copts took to bone so easily was that they had a long tradition of ivory carving. They continued to carve ivories during the Roman and Byzantine occupation of Egypt. These were probably too expensive to have been bought by ordinary Copts and were intended for export. Many of them have been found outside Egypt and they did a great deal to inspire Western ivory carvers during the Dark Ages. The kinds of bone objects which Copts made for their own use can be seen from the finds made in Coptic cemeteries. They include combs, pins for dressing women's hair, and pots for eye cosmetic.

Many of the Coptic bone carvings for furniture incorporate a vine leaf scroll with grapes, and a naked Cupid which may be either a Dionysian, or later a Christian symbol. These bone carvings are obviously related to similar work in ivory, which may show Nereids or other Hellenistic subjects. There are many bone and ivory carvings, many of them of the fifth century, which express pagan rather than Christian decorative ideas. It is difficult to relate Coptic bone art to Coptic ivory art, but it is possible to conjecture that the bone objects were intended for poor patrons, and that they may have been efforts by apprentices learning to work in ivory.

The legacy which the Copts bequeathed to their Arab supplanters in Egypt, to the art of Islam as a whole, and to the Christian West, was a very valuable one. When the Byzantines were thrown out of Egypt by the Arabs, the Copts were perfectly willing to labor for their new masters. They cooperated with their Arab rulers in decorating mosques and palaces. They went on carving bone plaques (there is a good set of them in the Louvre) in a style that differed little from that of Roman and Byzantine times. One change which the beliefs of the new rulers made essential was the removal of the naked Cupid—Islam deprecated the representation of living beings—but the vine remained, though by the time of the Arab Caliphate of the Omeyyades the design had become so stylized (as on the bone plaques preserved in the Berlin Museum) that this representation of the plant which provides wine—which was also anathema to the Muslims—could give no offense to true believers. It would take too long to discuss the dispersion of this essentially Coptic design of the vine branch and grapes and to speculate on how it appeared on the Mosque of Omar in Jerusalem and on the ivory throne of Maximianus, now in Ravenna, which were made, one in the seventh, the other in the sixth century. What can be said confidently is that it was from the Copts that the Arabs learned the use of the bone or ivory furniture plaque. As late as the tenth and eleventh centuries the Copts were still working alongside their Arab masters in amity: the age of severe persecution had not yet begun. Both races enjoyed an art which knew no religious differences, so that the decoration of the palaces of the Fatimid Caliphs, and of Coptic churches, such as Sitta Barbara, was virtually identical. On the most sumptuous pieces of furniture, such as the tenth-century lectern seen by A. J. Butler in the Coptic cathedral at Cairo, or the twelfth-century mosque pulpit or *mimbar* from a mosque in Cairo, now in the Victoria and Albert Museum, London, England, ivory plaques carved in floral decoration were inlaid into the wood. There can be no doubt, however, that bone was sub-

Plaque in bone, Coptic, seventh or eighth century. It shows the familiar vine scroll. ***Courtesy Victoria and Albert Museum, London, England.***

Coptic bone doll of the seventh or eighth century, which bears a faint and far-off resemblance to Parthian bone goddesses. *Courtesy Victoria and Albert Museum, London, England.*

stituted for the much more expensive ivory in all except the finest pieces of furniture.

Another Coptic bequest, to the West this time, was the "staring eye," the eyeball which is delineated by a deeply drilled hole. This staring eye may have been a copy, in the plastic arts, of the large eyes of the goddesses which appear so forcibly on the famous tapestries. It is possible to look for this staring eye through much of later bone carving, and to find it, for example, in the Whalebone Madonna. It may seem fanciful to attribute so strong an inspirational influence to Coptic art. Legacies from this source have a way of being overlooked, however. Let me give but one example. M. Jules Leroy, in the excellent introduction to *Ethiopia, Illuminated Manuscripts,*[1] makes the comment that the Ethiopian illuminator never hesitates to distort nature, particularly in "the constricted, contorted portraits of the Evangelists, with . . . their faces turned towards the spectator, their barely perceptible noses, and, above all, their wide, staring eyes."

It is true that the Ethiopian illuminator distorts faces, but the faces of the first four illuminations which Leroy reproduces have not been distorted by the illuminator of his own accord. They have been treated in exactly the same way that certain Coptic church wall hangings treat faces. An example of just this treatment can be found in a hanging now in Berne.[2] Seven centuries separate the hanging, which is seventh-century, from the manuscript, which is fourteenth-century. So far traveled, and long lasting, was Coptic art that its influence must be looked for where it is least expected.

One area where influence is to be expected is Arab Spain. There furniture marquetry inlay developed, based on the mosaics of Alexandria, which was called *taracea.* Bone carving, as well as ivory carving, was carried out in Andalusia, where a craftsman called Mohammed ben Assarach carved and dated a beautiful bone coffer ornamented with confronted greyhounds, at the beginning of the thirteenth century. It has been preserved in the Collegiate Church of San Isidore de Leon. Andalusian marquetry seems to show a preference for ivory over bone, and the use of sumptuous woods. I have stared long at the ceilings of the Alhambra in Granada, trying to determine whether the marquetry inlay units are bone or ivory. They certainly seem to be ivory, but it is difficult to tell.

Marquetry in the Andalusian style spread over North Africa, and gradually over the whole of the Muslim world. Nowhere did it find a more enthusiastic response than in Istanbul. Here Andalusian marquetry met and married the traditions of Turkish art which had been imported from Central Asia. The result was a great efflorescence of ornamental inlay work. As early as the fifteenth century special craft schools had been set up in the

1. M. Jules Leroy, *Ethiopia, Illuminated Manuscripts,* New York Graphic Society, UNESCO World Art Series (London 1961), p. 13.

2. P. M. du Bourguet, *Coptic Art* (London: Methuen, 1971), p. 55.

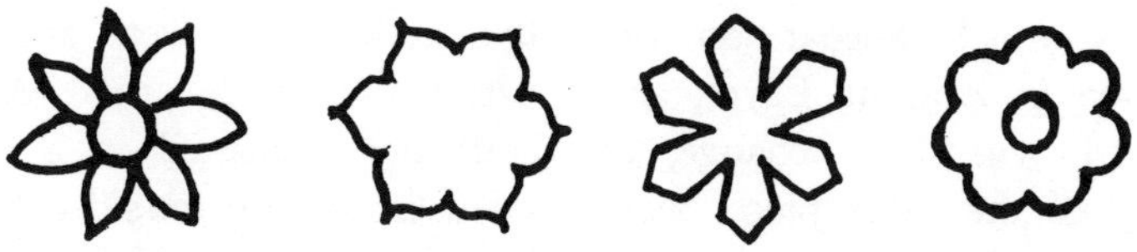

Traditional shapes for bone inlay used by Turkish *sedefjelar.*

Seraglio—the palace of the Sultan—to teach the art of inlaying silhouette inlay elements of bone, ivory, and mother of pearl in a dark wood base. By the seventeenth century more than 500 inlayers or *sedefjelar,* as they are called in Turkey, were working in Istanbul. They even had a special quarter assigned to them, near to the "burnt column," the collossal pillar of porphyry erected by the Emperor Constantine in the middle of the forum built by him. Close at hand was the Mosque of Ali Pasha, admired for the beauty of its facade, the elegance of its marble entrance, and its entablature, adorned with gilded inscriptions in calligraphy of the finest period.

Here they could be seen preparing the furniture and decorations which were to be fitted up in the royal palaces, or working on portable objects for sale. These small pieces included eight-legged octangular tables, on which were placed the trays of food from which Turkish diners helped themselves at a meal. Boxes of various sizes were also made, for locking up jewels, money, and papers. Small hand mirrors were made of cedar and a chestnut wood, inlaid with triangular or diamond-shaped pieces of inlay. Cradles with barge board ends, were also elaborately inlaid with inlay pieces of triangular and diamond shapes. In a harem which, even in its decline, housed 370 women, it is not surprising that there was a good deal of demand for cradles. Those made for the harem were carved in graceful openwork patterns, inlaid on both sides with the finest materials and studded with silver bosses, set with precious stones. Other small items produced by the *sedefjelar* included dust shovels into which the dust from the carpets upon which Turks reclined were swept. Particular skill was devoted to the production of *rakhla* or rests for the Koran. Everything concerning the holy book of Islam was treated with great seriousness by the Turks, who liked to claim that they had been exalted above other Muslims because of the respect which they showed for the Koran, so these reading desks are often masterpieces of the inlayer's art.

When not working in their studios, the inlayers labored on monumental constructions inside the palaces and mosques. These included paneling for the state galleys, the doors and ceilings of mausoleums, and the balustrades which surrounded the tombs of sultans and sultanas. The *sandooka* was a sort of bier which stood inside royal mausolea. It was an open, coffin-shaped frame, placed above the burial place of a sultan, and sometimes of a sultana Valide as well. Round about it ran a balustrade or *parmaklyk* made of cedar, richly carved and inlaid. Here the inlayer created some of his greatest triumphs, such as the balustrade which Sultan Mahmoud II placed round the bier of his daughter Saliha. Other masterpieces of the *sedefjelar* include the State Galley of Mehemet IV and the doors of the Erivan kiosk in the Seraglio.

It says much for the skill of the inlayer that so much work in a rather fragile art form should have survived. The ornamental elements were probably cut out with a saw, then sunk below the surface of the wood into compartments sculpted to receive them, or cemented together with other pieces shaped to fit them exactly. Occasionally they were sunk into a composition which hardened around them. Centuries of experience had taught the *sedefjelar* how to get the best out of a combination of just a few simple shapes. These shapes had evolved over the centuries; some of them had been brought by the Turks from Central Asia and recall Chinese art, others had been derived from the marquetry of Andalusia, some may be older still, such as the floral shapes which appear on the chair of Tutankhamen in Ancient Egypt, and which are reproduced. with little change, in Turkish inlay. Many of the inlay pieces were shaped like flowers: carnations, tulips, roses, and marguerites. Others were geometrical, such as the squares, hexagons, diamonds and circles which were so widely used. The irregular shapes had usually been inherited by the Turks from their Asiatic past; they consisted of flying dragons, crescents, chains, lanceheads and so forth.

Bone inlay work had early established itself in Persia. From Shiraz, in Persia, it reached Sindh, in India, about 1780, having been brought by three Multanis, Pershotum Hiralal and the brothers Devidas and Valeram. They taught many apprentices, and around 1810 the art was brought to Bombay by Manoredas, Nandhal, Lalchand, Thawardas, Rattanji, Pranvalab, and Narrondas. They trained a number of Parsee and Surat workers, who emigrated to Surat, Baroda, Ahmedabad, and elsewhere. In Bombay fifty masters, with about seventy-five apprentices, were at work in 1863. The patterns used by the "Ahmedhabad Work" craftsmen consisted of a round flower, a six-sided flower, a three-sided flower (which resembles that on Tutankhamen's chair) a rhombus-shaped flower, a square-sided flower, a small round pattern, called "silver bead" and another which combined all the materials used in inlay. The method by which the inlay was made up is described in Chapter Six. The materials consisted of stag horn, bone, ivory, left white or stained green, tin wire, sandal wood, ebony, and sappan wood.

Wherever ideas of Islamic inlay decoration had penetrated, a legacy was left for succeeding generations. The inlaid work of Girgenti and Salerno in Italy has a strong resemblance to that carried out in Bombay. Spanish inlaid furniture of the sixteenth century in the *mudejar* style, though using inlay shapes quite different from those in use in Arab Granada before the Conquest, nevertheless owes its origin to Muslim Arab craftsmen of Andalusia.

5

THE WHALEBONE MADONNA

European Carving from the Dark Ages to Romanesque Times

TO the watchers on the roofs of the fortresses which stood on lonely headlands, desolate islands, and isolated mountain tops across Scotland, the sight of whales disporting themselves in the warm waters near the shore must have been a familiar one. The Biscayan, the Humpback, the Fin, the Blue Whale, the Rorqual, the Sperm Whale, Cuvier's Whale, Sowerby's Whale and the Pilot Whale, were all regular visitors to Scottish waters.

Occasionally one of these monsters would come too far inshore, with results described in a poem written in the eighth century, and inscribed on one of the most famous of all whalebone carvings:

> He was dashed to death in his gambols,
> As aground he swam in the shallows.

Once sighted, the stranding of a whale would be eagerly reported to the local ruler, for, down to the present day, the whale reremains a royal fish. No whale caught or stranded in British waters can be claimed by anyone save the monarch. This royal prerogative, which aroused the democratic wrath of Herman Melville in the nineteenth century, had been established at a very early time because of the superior eating qualities of the whale. Whalemeat was considered a dish fit to set before a king. It appeared regularly at royal banquets in Scotland and England down to the sixteenth century, served up with seal, salted with the burnt ashes of seaware. Long after it had been abandoned by royalty, it continued to be eaten by less sophisticated folk, in the Orkneys, and outside of Scotland in the Faeroes.

Not even a barbaric king could eat a whole whale, however, so everyone in the neighborhood would rush in frenzied excitement to join in the feast, the men carrying knives, the women buckets, everyone running downhill towards the sea and shouting with excitement, as happens in the Faeroes when a school of pilot whales is stranded today. After the feast was over the bones of the whale would remain, raw material for the craftsman.

Whalebones, mixed with those of the seal and many other animals, have been found in the kitchen middens of fortresses in which the inhabitants of Scotland sheltered after the Romans left. These *brochs,* as they are called, were hollow stone towers sixty feet or more in height, riddled with galleries, and with the front door set sufficiently high up the wall to discourage casual visitors. They were inhabited by the Picts, who formed the inhabitants of northern and eastern Scotland, as a protection against their enemies, the Scots of the west and the English in the Kingdom of Northumbria to the south. The word "Pict" is the name the Romans had for them. It means "painted men," and came from the tattooed patterns with which they covered themselves from head to foot. It is fascinating to speculate that these tattoos may have been chiseled in with the tiny chisels made from seabird's wings which have been found in the *brochs.* The Maoris of New Zealand used bird bone chisels for tattooing, and it is difficult to think of any material, save human skin, which a bird bone chisel would cut. The Picts are the most mysterious race ever to have inhabited the British isles. We know almost nothing about them, except that they were great artists, much more talented than the Scots who eventually engulfed them. Before they disappear from history, however, they have bequeathed something of their artistic talent to the English of Northumbria, particularly in the skill of bone carving, and Pictish influences can still be seen in carved bone in England, down to the Norman Conquest.

Many people have argued that the Picts never occupied the *brochs* at all. Once again, it is their bone carving that gives the clue. In the *broch* of Burrian has been found the metatarsal bone of an ox, within incised symbols similar to those which appear on Pictish standing stones. The engraving on this piece of bone was probably practice undertaken before the pattern was cut into silver; down to Anglo-Saxon times at least, anyone carving in gold and silver cut his pattern first in bone. Many other objects of worked bone have been found in the *brochs,* denoting a well-developed technique. Buttons with iron shanks were fabricated from the outer table of its jawbone. Long-handled combs for weavers, and spindle whorls, were also cut from whalebone. Dice were made from sheep's shankbones and marked with tubular drills. Craftsmen excelled at making combs, which might be either very small, simple and delicately carved, barely big enough to hold between finger and thumb, or very large and elaborate, pieced together from several slabs of bone, riveted together, the teeth being cut out with a very fine saw. Once combs came to be used in the liturgical ceremonies of the Pictish church they became very heavily ornamented, as can be seen from the representation of one of them on a stone monument at Monifieth.

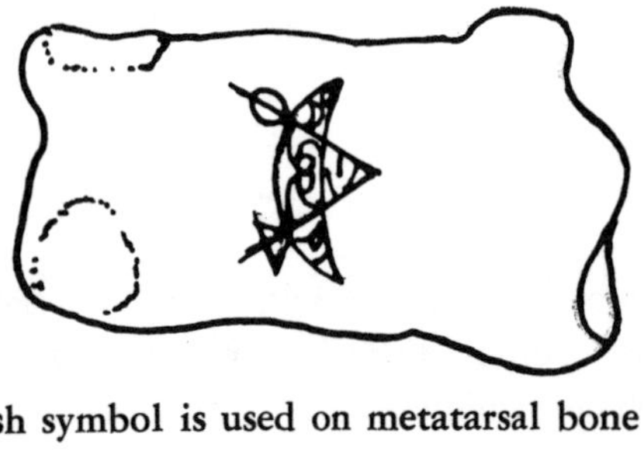

Pictish symbol is used on metatarsal bone of ox.

All the *broch* dwellers seem to have worn bone pins, no doubt to fasten together the plaids that were the principal garments of the time. These pins had ornamental heads, showing an incredible variety of design, in which the Scots thistle appears for the first time. Bone tools were innumerable, but nothing has been found in the *brochs,* or in the *crannogs* (artificial fortified islands set in the middle of lakes) to compare with what has come from another part of the Celtic world, Ireland.

Here, on the *crannogs* of Strokestown and Lagore, a few artists found peace and security amidst the turmoil that beset that country during the Dark Ages. They carried out incredibly versatile bone carvings, in which intricate designs formed from minute chip-carved recesses have been dotted, here and there, in haphazard fashion on the surface of a bone. This random placing of the pattern shows that the piece could never have been intended for display; it was practice carving for the finished work to be carried out in gold or silver. What was carved originally for a trial piece, however, may have been kept as a pattern book of ornament.

The lessons of Pictish and Celtic art were eagerly assimilated by the English, then prob-

Hawk from Pictish inscribed stone. Note spirals.

ably the greatest jewelers in Europe, who, like their northern neighbors, preferred to cut a trial pattern in bone first before beginning the final carving in silver or gold. The English were attentive and inspired craftsmen who used horn and bone for a multitude of purposes; combs, strap ends for buckles, hilts and handles of swords, linings of helmets, and of course for drinking horns for ale. These occupied an important place in English life, and no doubt in art as well. No ornamented drinking horns have survived (though the richness of the metal mountings which were fitted to them indicate how elaborate their decoration must have been). Nor have any of the horns blown in the chase or war survived.

There is not even a satisfactory picture of a drinking horn, except in the one representation of a Dark Age bone carver, a carving which shows Wayland Smith The Smith, a legendary English hero, making a drinking cup from an enemy's skull.

The carving of Wayland Smith occurs on one of the world's masterpieces of bone sculpture—The Franks Casket. This whalebone box (named after the benefactor who presented it to the British Museum) was made in Northumbria around 700 A.D. Carved on the sides of the box are inscriptions in very old English (the very earliest English ever to be written down dates from only twenty-five years before the box was made) written in runes, the alphabet used by the English and other northern peoples before they adopted Roman characters. Though no two scholars have ever translated the runes in the same way, all seem to agree that they are written in a dialect spoken north of the Humber, that is, in that part of Northumbria which bordered on the southern marches of Pictland. The way in which the box is carved shows that it was made by an artist deeply imbued with Pictish imagery and technique.

No one knows for certain what the box was meant to contain. It was probably intended for the jewels of some noble lady, but at some time in the middle ages it was taken to France, where it became part of the treasury of the Church of St. Julien de Brioude. There it stayed until the French Revolution, and when the church treasures were looted by the revolutionaries it passed into the hands of a bourgeois family at Auzon, near Brioude, one of whom tore off the silver mountings and fastenings which originally decorated it. This piece of vandalism was carried out so roughly that the panels of which the box was composed fell apart. Two of them disappeared completely, one of them wandered far from Auzon, the rest were bought by a local school teacher, who sold them to

The Franks Casket. "The Destruction Of Jerusalem." In the top right hand corner the artist has abandoned runes for the Roman alphabet and the legend reads: "HI FUGIUU NT HIERULIM" ("They flee from Jerusalem"). *Courtesy British Museum, London, England.*

The Franks Casket. Romulus and Remus and the She-Wolf are discovered. *Courtesy British Museum, London, England.*

The Franks Casket. Sigurd lies in his burial mound. Above ground are his horse, mourners talking of his deeds, and an animal-headed figure which shows the Pictish influence with which this carving is permeated. *Courtesy British Museum, London, England.*

The Franks Casket. Aegil defends his house. Note the single sweeping line which delineates the hair of the foremost assailants, a carving style derived from the Picts, which can be seen on their monuments. Note too the "exploded" stockade with its battlements, which has opened out like a folding paper model. Aegil's wife crouches between the High Seat pillars of the house, ready to supply her husband with fresh arrows as he shoots them out of loopholes in the walls at his enemies. Heroism was expected of both men and women in Anglo-Saxon England, and this carving is a reminder to the noble lady who owned the box of where her duty lay—to defend her home to the last. *Courtesy British Museum, London, England.*

The Franks Casket. On the left, Wayland Smith. On the right, the "Adoration of the Magi." Note the peculiar spiral which attaches the wings of the swans on the left to their bodies. This is a Pictish touch. *Courtesy British Museum, London, England.*

The Franks Casket. The side facing the reader shows Wayland Smith making a cup from the skull of an enemy. Note the cable twist border, a motif which was still being employed by whalebone carvers aboard American whalers in the nineteenth century. *Courtesy British Museum, London, England.*

Goose from Franks Casket. Note spiral where wing joins body.

a Paris dealer, from whom they were bought by Sir Augustus Franks, who presented them to the British Museum in 1867.

The other surviving panel was bought by a French collector, who bequeathed it to the Bargello Museum in Florence, where it has remained ever since. It seems no attempt has ever been made by the British Museum authorities to recover it, though no doubt the National Museum in Florence would be perfectly prepared to exchange this English masterpiece in return for one or two Florentine works of art, of which there are a great many in English collections.

The box is made up of sizable slabs of bone, about nine inches long sawn from the jawbone, or possibly the shoulder blade, of a whale. The carver has recorded how he collected the raw material himself:

> The whale's bones from the fishes' floods,
> I lifted on Fergen Hill.

This tiny bone carving appears to be related to the school of the Franks Casket. Note how the hair of the figures is divided into ridges, as is that of one of the figures in the Aegil scene. *Courtesy Victoria and Albert Museum, London, England.*

It was apparently quite normal for bone carvers to collect their raw material in the field in this way right through the middle ages. In a manuscript written in the latter part of the twelfth century, a Scottish bone carver is described as traveling through the forest, in search of the antlers of a stag which has been hunted and killed there, carrying with him his tools to cut them up.

It seems very probable that whoever carved the whalebone sides of the cask box also made the silver lock clasps and hinges which once fastened it. This would seem to be indicated by the carving of Wayland The Smith, who is represented as a bone carver but a smith as well. He holds in his hands a cup, fashioned from the skull of one of his enemies, but around him stand the tools belonging to an armorer and goldsmith, forge, fire, and tongs, while on the wall hang armor and weapons which he has made. Needless to say, this armor was not plain hammered metal, but, in accordance with the fashion of the day, was heavily ornamented and inlaid with gold and silver. No doubt Wayland cut out all his gold and silver carving in bone first. The box has obviously been designed by a jeweller. Blank spaces have been carefully left in the whalebone surface wherever they are necessary for the clasps and hinges. When we remember that the box was probably intended as a jewel case, or *theca,* as they were called at the time, it does not seem unlikely that the person who carved the whalebone and made the goldsmithery were one and the same. One can almost hear the craftsman ask, as he sells some jewels to a lady, "Perhaps you would like a box to put them in?"

The choice of the images carved on the box has puzzled art historians very much. Unable to relate this unique masterpiece to anything similar, they soon got out of their depth, like the whale at Fergen Hill; not being artists themselves they have found it impossible to conceive how an artist's mind works.

The surviving panels of the box consist of scenes drawn from pagan Norse legend: the smithy of Wayland, the burial of Sigurd, and Aegil defending his house, all subjects probably familiar to readers of Anglo-Saxon poetry, which drew largely on the legends of Teutonic Europe as a whole, but which has only survived in a fragmentary state.

The artist could apparently read Old English in runic lettering, because he has carved his runes superbly. He also apparently knew some Latin and could carve in the Roman alphabet, though he is not so fond of this as he is of runes. It is not surprising, then, that he includes images from the Bible and world history. They include: the Adoration of the Magi, Romulus and Remus, and Titus' capture of Jerusalem. Faced with this unusual combination of subjects, some critics have not hesitated to dismiss the subject matter of the box as an unrelated hodgepodge, though it ought to be pointed out that the fact that the box is incomplete may have added to our difficulties in interpreting it. Possibly the missing panels contained an inscription which gave the key to the whole composition.

Just as puzzling in its way as the choice of images is the way in which they are treated. Although the artist is a master carver of pictures, he is so much in love with lettering that he has cut down the size of his pictures to make room for more lettering. Just half the width of the sides of the box have been allocated to the inscriptions in runes. He imposes his own rules of art on reality and they must be understood before his work can be appreciated fully. Thus, in defiance of perspective, the whole of the stockade surrounding Aegil's house, with its battlements, is opened out and spread flat, as if an explosion had suddenly knocked all the walls down. Similarly, Romulus and Remus, lying flat on the ground sucking the teats of the she-wolf, appear to be kicking their heels in the air.

The technique involved in the carving is strikingly unusual. The top of the carved surfaces stands out flat, with almost no surface modeling, like the face of a wood block. The whole of the spaces devoted to sculpture has been filled with figures, buildings, foliage, ornamental dots, and more runes. The panels devoted to the runic inscriptions, however, show all the runic letters carefully backed by blank spaces. The *horror vacui* (hatred of an empty space) which characterizes the carving of the pictures has been explained as characteristic of barbaric art. The true explanation (there are many barbaric carvings of the period with many blank surfaces, such as the Pictish stone monuments) is that the pictures were much easier to carve by using an incision technique than if they were filled up with lots of images. By using a technique of this sort the artist would have to remove a smaller amount of whalebone—and whalebone is a hard material to carve. The runes had to be left with a blank background to make them visible. A flat surface with a sunk down background is moreover characteristic of some of the Pictish monuments, such as the Aberlemno Cross, or the sculptured stones of St. Vigeans. Other resemblances to Pictish imagery which have escaped notice so far are the single line from the forehead to the back of the neck which delineates the hair and the spirals on the wings of the birds which Aegil is killing. Spirals such as these are to be found on the leg-and-body junctions of certain famous Pictish animal engravings, such as the bird on the Easterton of Roseisle stone and the Burghead Bulls. Other resemblances between the whalebone carving and Pictish art have been commented on in the past; they include animal headed figures, similar to those which appear on the Pictish stone at Inchbrayock, and the framing of the she-wolf in the Romulus scene between the branches of the tree, which can be paralleled by the treatment of a deer on a Pictish sarcophagus in St. Andrews.

If so much of the Franks Casket is Pictish, what English element remains in one of the greatest of English sculptures?

Apart from minor details, such as the flaunting headlines of the runes, which form such a marked contrast to the timid and sporadic use of lettering in Pictish monuments, the whole composition breathes a spirit apparently completely alien to Pictish thought, but one which was very close to the English outlook of the time—hero worship. Take the choice of subjects for example: Aegil defends his home at odds of seven to one, Sigurd, asleep in his burial mound, lives on, after death, in the stories of his brave deeds that the group standing by the mound recall to one another, after a siege whose epic qualities retold in some world chronicle found a welcoming note in the heart of the English carver, the last defenders of Jerusalem escape from the captured city, Romulus and Remus drink in, with the milk of their foster mother, the she-wolf, the spirit which is to inspire Rome, Wayland wreaks vengeance on his enemies among the arms which he has forged for heroic warriors, while his brother Aegil works on a device to help him confound his foes, and finally the Magi bring their long and dangerous journey to its appointed conclusion.

Commentators on the box may be more easily forgiven for failing to recognize the relating theme of the subjects it figures (a theme which was no doubt emphasized by the now-missing inscriptions and images on the lid of the box) than for recognizing the connection between the carver himself and the most prominent hero figure on the casket who is placed so that whoever opens the box must see him. This is, of course, Wayland, himself a bone carver, like the maker of the Franks Casket, because he is working up a human skull into a drinking cup. Whether commissions of this sort frequently fell to bone carvers of early English times is difficult to say, but just a little later, the Vikings were accused of drinking ale from the skulls of their enemies.

Heroic subjects such as these would have found a sympathetic response from contemporary English folk. At the time the casket was made their literature was just beginning to be written down for the first time. Much of it has been lost, but if nothing had survived

Anglo-Saxon chessmen in whalebone (left to right) Knight, Pawn, Bishop. *Courtesy British Museum, London, England.*

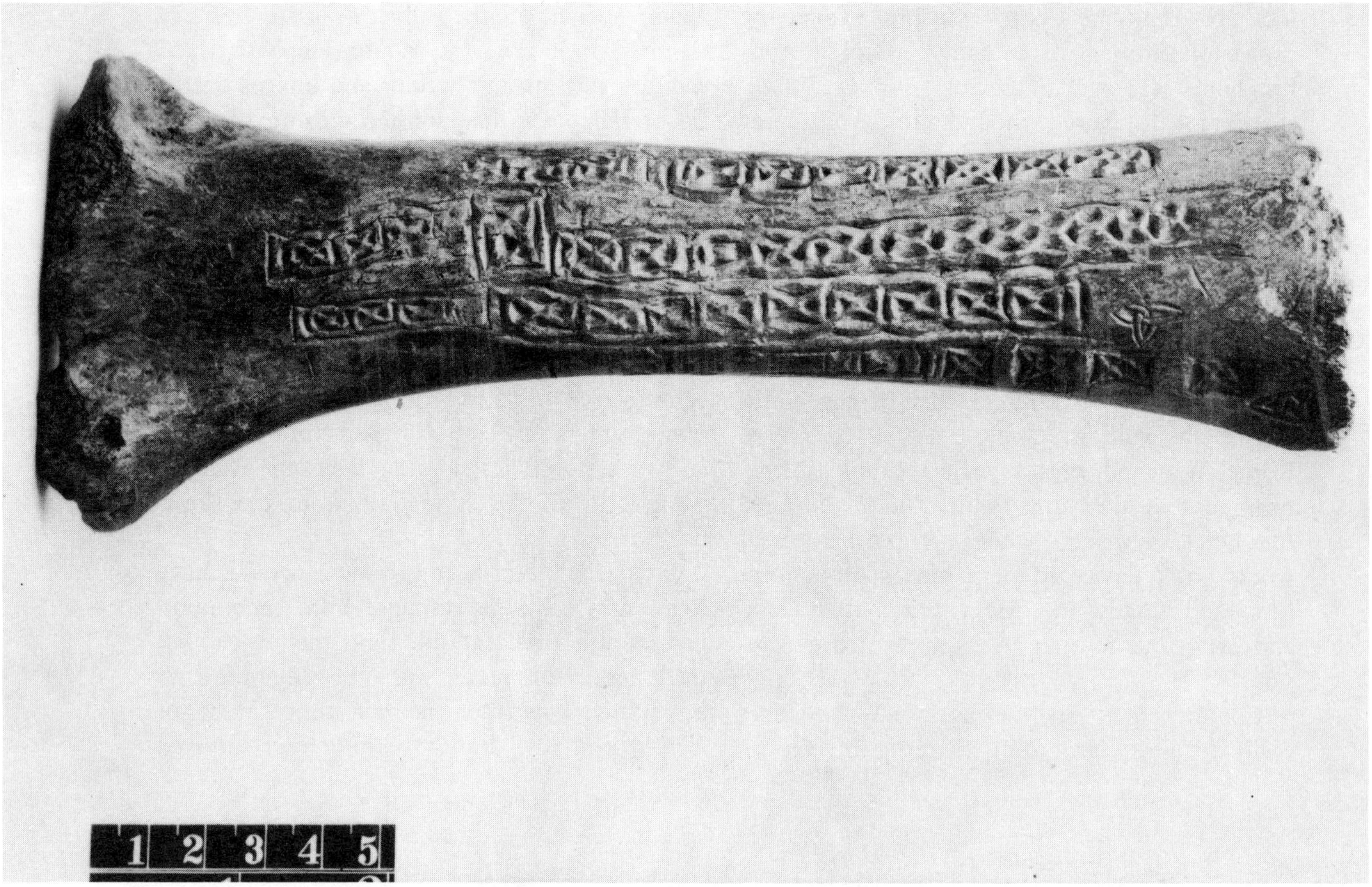

Anglo-Saxon trial carvings made on an animal bone, preparatory to carving gold or silver. ***Courtesy British Museum, London, England.***

save the poem which describes how Beowulf, the St. George of pagan England, goes out to fight his last battle with the dragon there would still be enough in which to recognize a spirit of heroism akin to that which we find on the panels of the Franks Casket, which was carved about the same time that "Beowulf" was written. It is not difficult to imagine that, while she selected her jewels from the box, a noble Northumbrian lady might talk to the children clustered round her, and tell them what would be expected of them in later life, using the images on the box as examples.

Heroism continued to be a quality much in demand in Anglo-Saxon England, as Northumbria fell beneath the onslaught of the combined Scots and Danes. Although Northumbria had disappeared, Northumbrian art—or something of its quality—survived, and whalebone carving progressed in ingenuity and technical finish, even if these qualities can now be recognized only in the minor pieces, strap ends, buckles, and so forth, which have survived. Around the year 894, King Alfred, ruler of Wessex, the only English kingdom to have survived the onslaught of the Vikings, and a great patron of art, who kept the best craftsmen at court and had them work under his eye, made extensive notes about the sources of those essential raw materials of art, whalebone and walrus ivory.

Othere, a Norwegian trader who had visited him, said that where he lived, at Helgeland, whales were extremely plentiful. He had killed as many as sixty-six in three days.[1] These

1. King Alfred, *The Anglo Saxon Version from the Historian Orosius, by Alfred the Great,* W. Bowyer and J. Nichols (London, 1773).

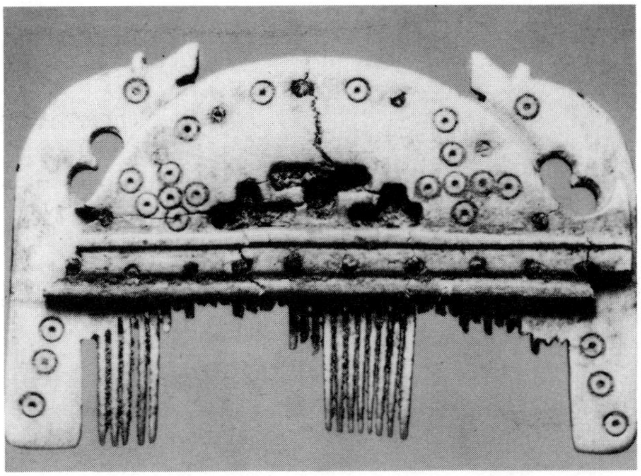

Anglo-Saxon bone comb of the sixth or seventh century. ***Courtesy Victoria and Albert Museum, London, England.***

whales measured six and three quarters times as much as a walrus, so they were probably blue whales, or common Rorquals. Othere's Finnish tenants, who herded reindeer in the long narrow province of Helgeland, which was bounded on one side by the sea, on the other by wild moors, paid him their rent partly in whalebone. Othere had brought some walrus tusks as a present to the King, suggesting that there must have been some ivory and bone carvers at court, otherwise they would have been of little use to him.

Not all Alfred's visitors from Scandinavia were as peaceful as Othere. He spent his whole life fighting off the raids of the Vikings, ferocious pirates who had overrun half of England and completely disrupted overseas trade. Supplies of ivory had probably failed completely, making substitutes for ivory, such as whalebone, walrus tusks, and other bone and horns more desirable.

Besides trading whalebone from the northern seas to England, the Vikings had affected bone carving in other ways. They were famous for personal cleanliness in an unwashed age. Not only did they take a bath every Saturday (called "bath day" in old Norse) but they frequently combed their hair. All this, says a contemporary Englishman, was done to "undermine the chastity of Englishwomen and seduce the daughters of noble ladies." A few of their splendid horn combs, ornamented with strapwork copied from Celtic originals, have survived.

By the end of the Viking period the rather stay-at-home Anglo-Saxons had become infected by the adventurous spirit of their invaders, and they too had taken up whaling. There is a reference to the first English whalers, the Ahabs and Starbucks of their day, in, of all sources, a handbook for Latin conversation, written by Aelfric, Abbot of Ensham, some time before 1000, for the use of his pupils. "Do you want to capture a whale?" the master asks, to which the pupil is supposed to reply "No." The master asks why not, and the boy replies: "Because whaling is dangerous. It is safer for me to go to the river with my ship than to go hunting the whale with many ships."[2] "Nevertheless," the master replies "Many people do capture whales and escape the dangers."

It is perhaps worth mentioning that the Lapps, who are of the same race as Othere's Finnish tenants, seem to have been influenced in the present day fashions which they wear by Viking clothing of the Saga period. Modern-day Lapps are not merely fine bone carvers, they also carry about with them examples of their handicraft, in the shape of the horn-topped walking stick, and the reindeer antler sheath for knives. Both of these pieces of personal gear may have some connection with Viking work.

Viking work in horn and bone has survived in some quantity. The Vikings hunted elks, deer, reindeer, whales, walrus, and seal. Bone and horn provided a cheap and handy material in which to make objects of everyday life, such as the pleating board of whalebone found at Birka, and also artistic and decorated objects, such as the brilliant carving of a Viking's head in elk horn, found at Sigtuna, which was made in the eleventh or twelfth century.

Viking handicrafts such as horn carving were carried out in trading towns such as Haithabu, Birka, Sigtuna, and Helge. The work done was varied. Objects required by householders included weaving combs (which were

2. Aelfric, *Colloquium,* Book 1, Chapter 1, p. 13.

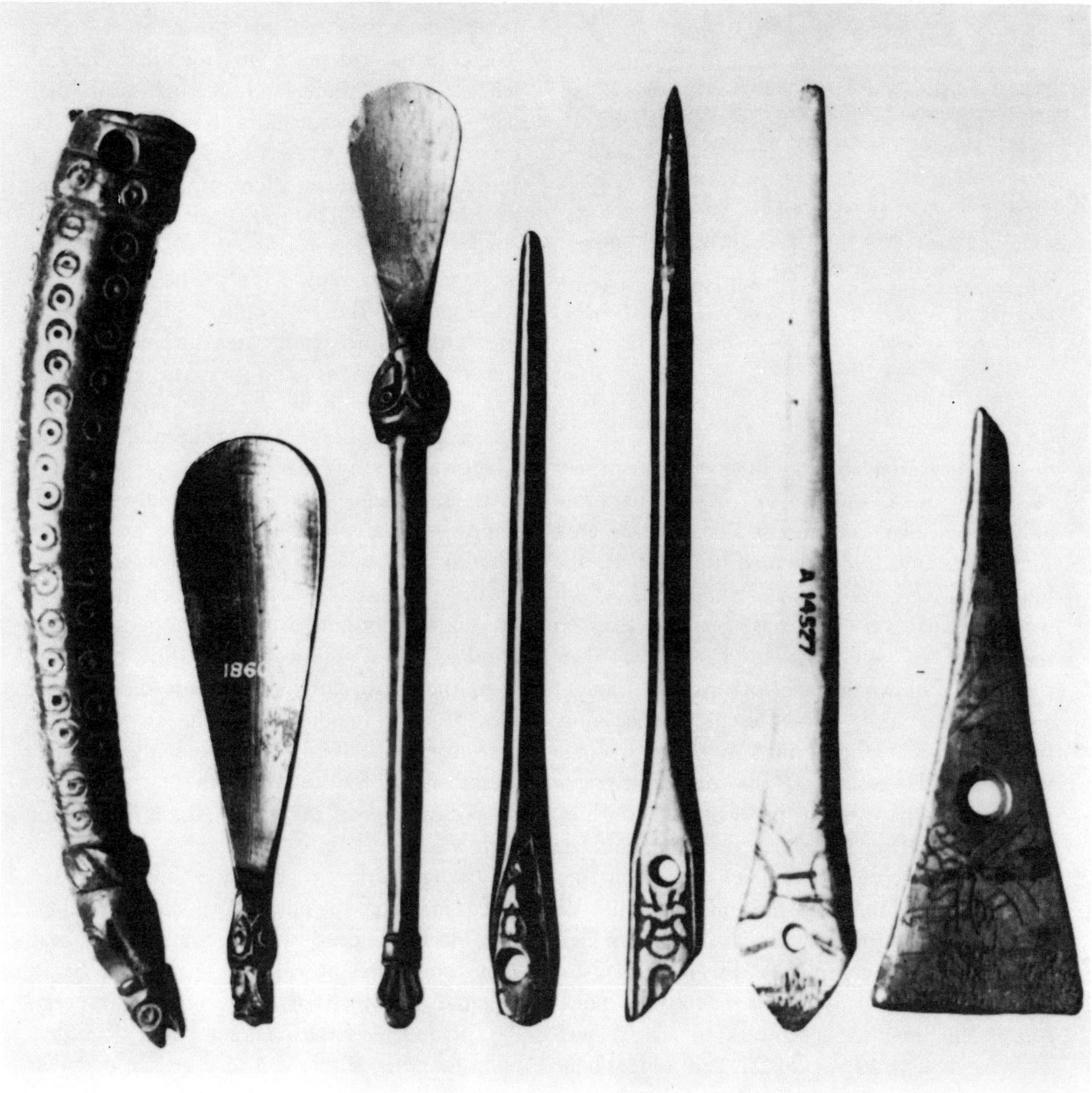

Bone pins and spoons with engraving in Ringerike style and a horn handle with an animal head from Viking remains found in London. *Courtesy London Museum, Kensington Palace, London, England.*

Scottish bone draughtsman, eleventh century. *Courtesy Victoria and Albert Museum, London, England.*

Anglo-Saxon bone carving of the eleventh century depicting Christ in Majesty, found in the rectory garden (formerly the site of a nunnery) at Leckhampton, Buckinghamshire, England. *Courtesy Victoria and Albert Museum, London, England.*

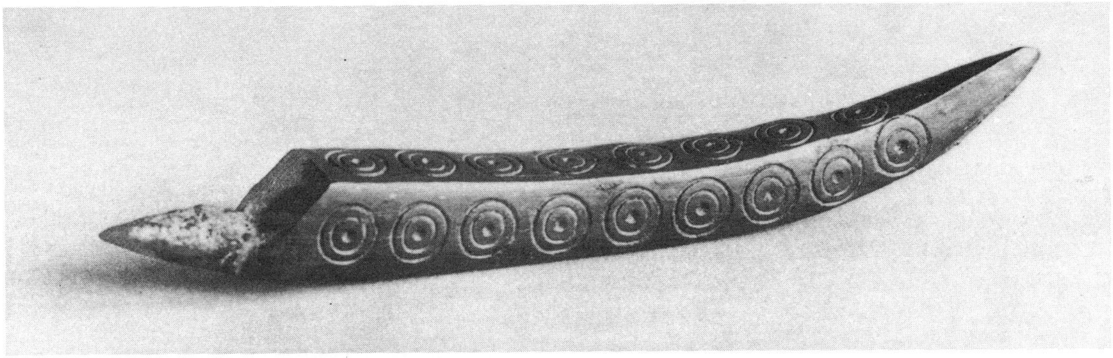

Viking bone carving, perhaps a netting shuttle, or the top of a walking stick. *Courtesy Victoria and Albert Museum, London, England.*

very like the combs used in contemporary India, and which may have had a common, Indo-European origin) spoons, which might be ornamented with a very sophisticated interlocking hollow diamond pattern, and ornaments for ladies, such as combs which were ingeniously made in four pieces, the front of the crown, the back of the crown, and two toothed pieces, all fitted together with copper rivets, and looking rather like the Pictish combs which I mentioned earlier, from which indeed they may have been copied. Pins, some with square heads, some with open work heads, were also in demand for ladies' coiffures. Warriors ordered sword beaters, such as that found at Stong Tjersadalier in Iceland, and possibly bone handles for swords as well.

Besides being clever craftsmen, the Vikings were addicted to board games. So that they could go on playing, even on the tossing

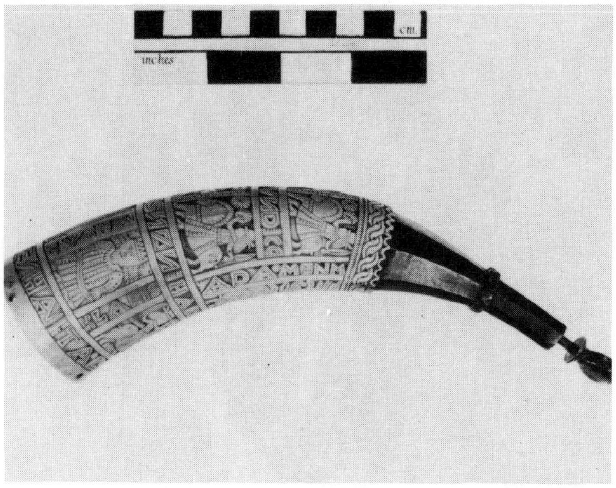

Scandinavian powder horn, seventeenth or eighteenth century. ***Courtesy Tower of London, London, England.***

Another view of the same powder horn. ***Courtesy Tower of London, London, England.***

deck of a ship at sea, they ingeniously constructed bone draughtsmen, drilled with holes in the middle, so that they could be placed on pegs set in a draughtsboard. Boards for their national game of *tafl* were made from whalebone with a special handle, on each side of the board, to be held by a player while the two contestants sat side by side on a sea chest. Holes were drilled in the board, and pegs inserted into the *tafl* pieces so they could be pegged securely to the board at each move.

The Vikings had also enthusiastically taken up a new board game, chess, which had just been introduced into Europe. The earliest European sets had been made for the Arabs who had invaded Spain, during the first quarter of the eighth century. The game had been invented in India many centuries before, and the sets made there, and in Persia, had been naturalistic in design. The King had been a real king, sitting in a howdah on top of an elephant, the Knight had been a horse and so on. Realistic portrayals of men or animals was quite contrary to Muslim religious ideas, however, so the Muslim Arabs drastically altered the shapes of the pieces, making them into abstract gamesmen, which nonetheless sometimes still bore a far-away resemblance to the originals. Thus the Knight, which had been a horse, still had a rather blunt face which pushed forward. These small abstract shapes lent themselves admirably to being made up in bone, whereas the old pieces had been so large, and so elaborate, that they could only be successfully portrayed in a block of ivory. Chess sets, first of Arab manufacture, then of Viking make, began to circulate through Europe.

The Anglo-Saxon carvers and the Viking craftsmen, who had now settled peacefully amongst them, produced whalebone chess sets, bone knife handles, combs, buttons, and pins, as well as ornamental plaques carved from bone, such as a splendid one of two confronted gryphons. Continental craftsmen, full of the new ideas sweeping across Europe, but also knowledgable about the best of the old ivory carvings, such as the Roman diptychs and Carolingian and Ottonian book covers treasured in monastic libraries, added a new leaven to English carving.

The two varied streams of inspiration run together in what is probably the most famous of all English medieval carvings, the "Adoration of the Magi." The title of this late eleventh-century carving, now in the Victoria and Albert Museum, London, is, like other museum titles, something of a misnomer. The Magi do enter into the composition, but only as timid visitors, crammed into about a third of the available space, who tip-toe timidly into the presence of the Virgin. Not only are the Magi allotted a smaller area than

Viking and medieval gaming pieces. Note how the Viking pieces have a hole pierced in the middle so that they can be placed on top of a peg protruding from a gaming board. Pieces of this sort were obviously intended for playing aboard ship. *Courtesy London Museum, Kensington Palace, London, England.*

German Romanesque chessman in stag's horn.

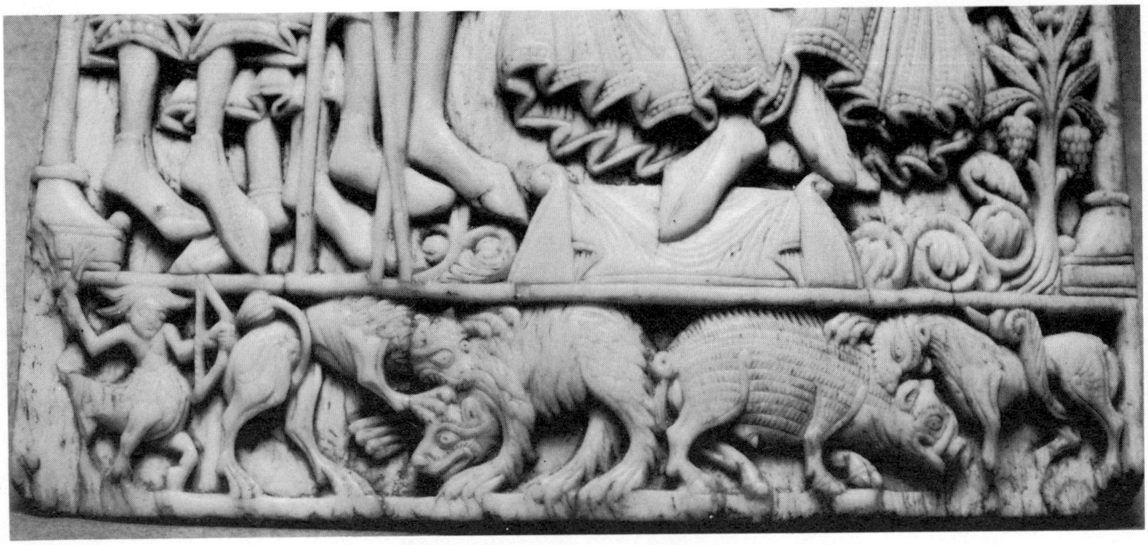

Detail from the "Adoration of the Magi," now considered to be late eleventh century and English. Note the centaur archer. *Courtesy Victoria and Albert Museum, London, England.*

Detail of the "Adoration of the Magi." Note the abrupt finish of the carving once the last architectural stage is reached, suggesting that this sculpture of the Virgin really is "A Tower of Ivory." *Courtesy Victoria and Albert Museum, London, England.*

"Adoration of the Magi." *Courtesy Victoria and Albert Museum, London, England.*

in any other comparable rendering of the Adoration, but the artist has emphasized their downcast eyes, and the feeling of conscious humility which has pulled down the corners of their mouths. The Virgin, cleverly made to seem gigantic in spite of the small size of the carving, dominates the scene. The hypertrophic and cross-eyed glare with which she regards her adorers owes a good deal to the difficulty of the carver in carving faces. He has found it impossible to give her face sufficient depth; the bad modeling of the nostrils can be paralleled in other carvings of the period, but he has also managed to lay out the base of the nose, the groove of the upper lip, and the line of the mouth at wrong angles to the center line of the face. Far from destroying the success of the carving, these little blemishes positively enhance it, because they give the Virgin a compelling, hypnotic look which holds the glance of the spectator, almost against his will. Was the difficulty felt by the carver in sculpting the Virgin's face owing to the fact that he was a monastic artist who had never seen a woman's face?

It is always the obvious that is overlooked in art. No one has commented on the fact that the artist was happier at creating minute repetitive ornaments than faces or figures, nor on the peculiar shape of the carving. Only part of the radius, or fore fin, of a Rorqual, or Finner whale, has been used for the work, so the size, and shape, of the composition must have been deliberately chosen. Most bone or ivory carvings are square, oblong, or cross shaped, with just a few carved in the shape of a mandorla. As it stands, the carving does not seem designed to fit in with others, as part of a fitted-together scheme of carvings. The idea that it might have been made as a box lid must be dismissed because the underside has not been smoothed.

If the shape of the carving has no practical significance, might it not have a symbolic one? Here, if ever, is a direct translation of liturgical expression into plastic form.

Romanesque bone coffer, carved with scenes from the Romance of Tristram and Iseult. ***Courtesy British Museum, London, England.***

Romanesque bone coffer, carved with scenes from the Romance of Tristram and Iseult, another view. *Courtesy British Museum, London, England.*

Byzantine bone casket of the tenth century, detail. *Courtesy Victoria and Albert Museum, London, England.*

Byzantine bone box of the tenth century. Note the rosettes and classical influence. *Courtesy Victoria and Albert Museum, London, England.*

Byzantine bone casket of the tenth century. Note the flower-shaped rosettes and the strong classical inspiration which relate this box to the Veroli Casket (p. 71). *Courtesy Victoria and Albert Museum, London, England.*

Bone and ivory Byzantine coffer of the tenth century. The vine scroll may be derived from a Coptic model. *Courtesy Victoria and Albert Museum, London, England.*

Veroli Casket, detail. ***Courtesy Victoria and Albert Museum, London, England.***

The Virgin, standing in an architectural framing which suggests a building, and in which the narrowing of the carving has cleverly suggested, by false perspective, an edifice towering above the beholder, and formed of white, gleaming, whalebone, is a "Tower of Ivory," or *turris eburnea.* This is just the term, borrowed from Scripture, with which she is hailed in contemporary liturgical works.

No other carvings approach the Virgin, even remotely, in force and majesty. It is true that there is another whalebone Virgin and Child in the Louvre in Paris, a Spanish carving of the twelfth century, which has familiar suggestions in the protruding eyes, heavily underlined eye cavity, gauffered coif, and the position of the child. A South Italian bone box of the twelfth century, also in the Victoria and Albert, shows a Byzantine skill and technical finesse which characterize the "Adoration of the Magi" as well. Other notable bone carvings of the period, such as two English book cover plaques of the second quarter of the twelfth century, also in the Victoria and Albert, are striking by the mere fact that they offer no comparisons.

Manuscripts, stone reliefs, wood carvings, architectural details, and ivory carvings, have been called on as evidence that the "Adoration of the Magi" was carved in England, Ireland, the Low Countries, Normandy, Spain, or the shores of the English Channel. Recently the probability of a southern English workshop has been learnedly argued. There are resemblances between the Adoration and two Anglo-Saxon ivory carvings of the eleventh century, one an ivory box in the Victoria and Albert, the other a pencase in the British Museum, both made from walrus ivory. The resemblances evoked are details—the way in which draperies are arranged, the manner in which fighting monsters are pictured. Any search for

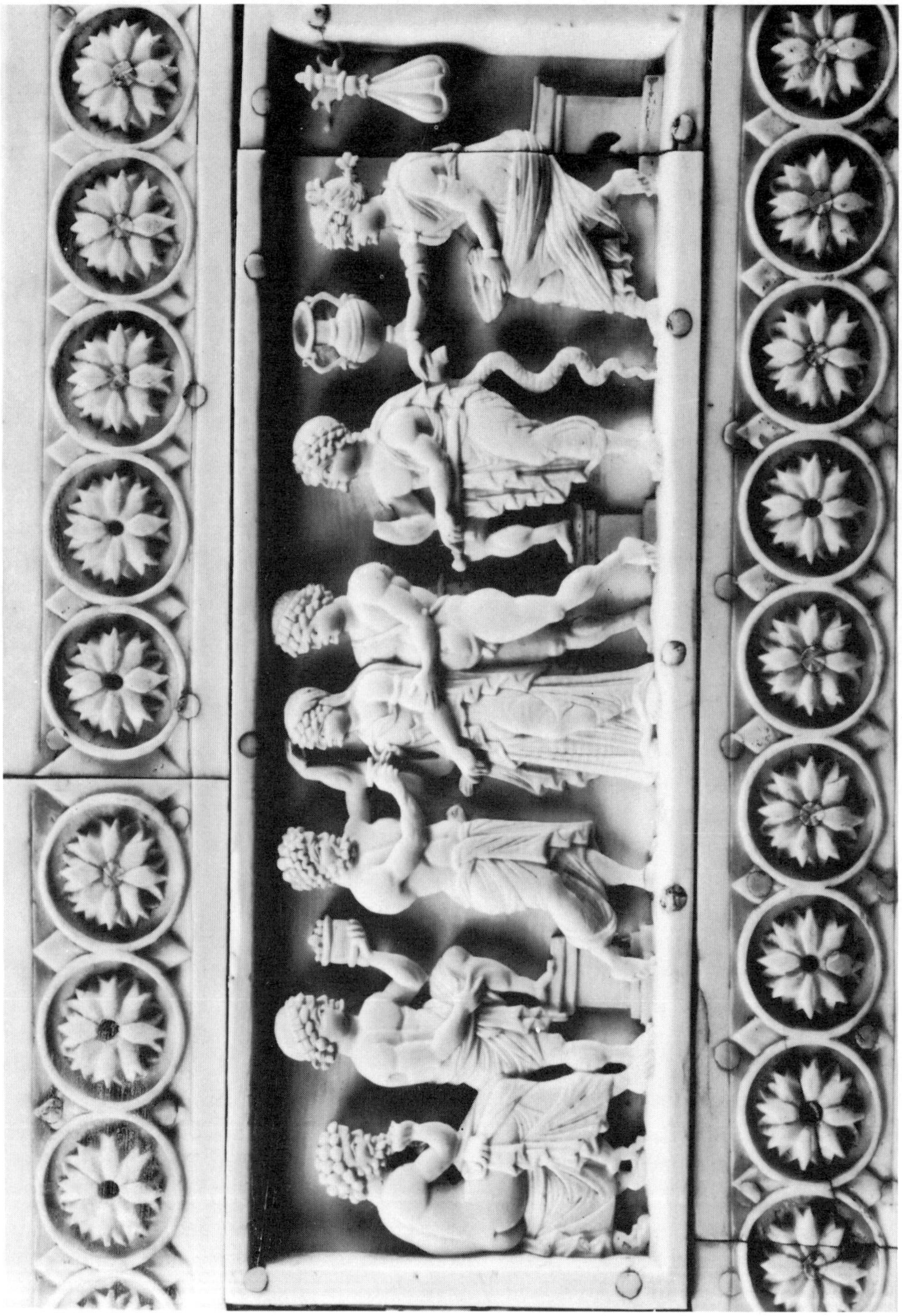

Veroli Casket, detail. *Courtesy Victoria and Albert Museum, London, England.*

Veroli Casket, detail. *Courtesy Victoria and Albert Museum, London, England.*

Veroli Casket, detail. *Courtesy Victoria and Albert Museum, London, England.*

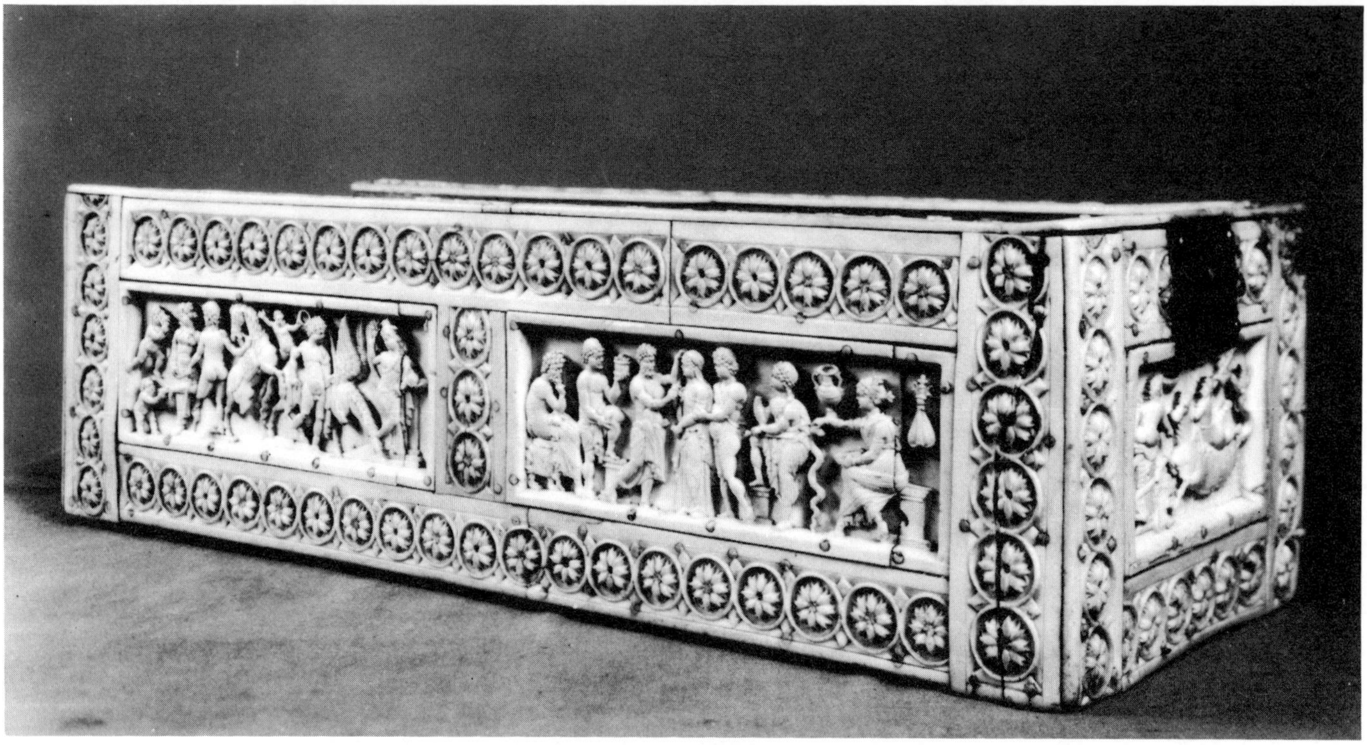

The Veroli Casket, a late tenth or early eleventh-century Byzantine box of bone and ivory. In spite of its late date the inspiration of the casket is almost wholly classical. Its existence pre-supposes the existence of many bone and ivory carvings made in late Roman times (probably in Alexandria) which were continuously copied throughout the Middle Ages. *Courtesy Victoria and Albert Museum, London, England.*

the origins of the "Adoration of the Magi" must be directed to matters of detail, because it is obvious that if any representation of the main parts of the composition survived, it would have been discovered by now. In any case detail is of immense significance in determining the relationship of one carver to another. An African ivory carver, like Marko Scott of Blantyre, Malawi, for example, carves the eyes of his birds in a particular way, exactly in the way he was taught to carve them by his master in the art, Jackson Sadiq.

Curiously enough the most significant detail of the Adoration has been overlooked. This is the Centaur carrying a bow and arrow at the base of the plaque. This is the only centaur archer which appears on any ivory carving, so far as I know, save for one other piece. This is a walrus ivory box, of English workmanship, related to St. Albans and probably made about 1120. It is carved with centaurs carrying bows and arrows and, significantly, dressed in girdles of leaves, like the centaur on the whalebone plaque. Fighting centaurs have a long history in British art. One carrying two axes appears on the Aberlemno stone. A carver in walrus ivory such as those working at St. Albans would be particularly well trained to carve whalebone. Walrus, unlike elephant ivory, has a hard, solid, yet spongy mass in the center. Only the outside is really workable. A carver in these materials, then, as in bone, has to accomodate himself to a shallow depth of raw material.

Pierced bone plaques, probably intended to be used as the ornaments for book covers. Note the resemblance between the layout of the ornament and that on a contemporary Romanesque bone coffer, now in the Victoria and Albert Museum as well. These book covers are now considered to be English, and are dated from the second quarter of the twelfth century. ***Courtesy Victoria and Albert Museum, London, England.***

There seems no reason, then, to refrain from claiming the "Adoration of the Magi" for what it is, the last masterpiece of English bone carving emanating from the shrine of England's first saint St. Albans. The English school had not been wholly indigenous; as has been seen it had incorporated classical motifs, such as centaurs, freely into its work. It had even borrowed details of classical ivory carvings, such as acanthus leaves, beading, palm trees, and floral embroideries, all of which, no doubt, were ultimately derived from consular diptychs. At its most derivative, however, it had still been markedly individual. This individuality, characterized by work such as the charming little "Virgin and Child" in the British Museum, disappears after the Norman Conquest; English workmanship is swallowed up by the main Continental School.

Before leaving the Romanesque period, brief mention must be made of the portable altars executed by Romanesque carvers in whalebone.

Coffer made in bone of the Romanesque period. Note the resemblance between this coffer and the book cover reproduced beside it. ***Courtesy Victoria and Albert Museum, London, England.***

Strictly speaking, every altar, whether portable or not, should have been of stone. However, an exception seems to have been made, readily, for whalebone, and much later on, bone altars are made by the Embriachi. A fine example of a whalebone altar (now in America) is composed of four oblong whalebone plaques, which have been re-mounted as a box, with a modern wooden base and hinged lid. At one end of the altar Christ appears in majesty within a mandorla, at the other end the Crucifixion is represented. The two long sides are carved with standing figures of the twelve Apostles, carried out in a style similar to that of English stone sculpture of the second quarter of the twelfth century. The figures show a resemblance to those on the frieze of the West Front of Lincoln Cathedral, which was altered by Bishop Alexander, between 1123 and 1148. Another altar, so similar in style as to postulate an identical workshop, is in the British Museum.

Another of the pair of pierced bone plaques. *Courtesy Victoria and Albert Museum, London, England.*

Walrus ivory box, considered to be English and related to St. Albans, where it may have been made about 1120. Compare the centaur archer with that on the Whalebone Madonna (p. 66). Armed centaurs also appear on the Pictish monuments. *Courtesy Victoria and Albert Museum, London, England.*

End of Romanesque portable altar in whalebone, showing Christ in a Mandorla, surrounded by the symbols of the Four Evangelists. Twelfth century. *Courtesy British Museum, London, England.*

The other end of the twelfth century Romanesque whalebone altar, showing the Crucifixion. *Courtesy British Museum, London, England.*

A Romanesque whalebone portable altar of the twelfth century, intended to be carried on journeys or voyages. This view shows six of the Twelve Apostles. *Courtesy British Museum, London, England.*

6

HORNS WINDING FAINTLY

Late Medieval Carving

ONLY distant echoes of what must have been the most elaborately carved and highly prized pieces of horn carving, the horn itself, have reached us. Only fragments of bugle horns have survived, but enough has been left to show what we have lost. To a medieval gentleman a hunting horn was a mark of status, like a knight's spurs. To be able to blow, or "wind" any of the many varied calls was the mark of the polished courtier, as opposed to the rustic squire. Minute directions are given in medieval treatises on hunting for sounding the different calls blown at particular stages of the chase. When, for example, the stag had been driven from his hiding place in the bracken, the huntsman blew *Il est haut* a call that has come down to us as "Tally Ho!" The bugle horn, as depicted in medieval manuscripts, was either the shape of a bull's horn (the word "bugle" means "a young ox") or it was crescent shaped. It was slung by a leather strap over one shoulder and rested on the opposite hip. It was blown in an almost perpendicular position, the wide mouth piece curving well above the huntsman's head. The tablature, or music for hunting horns which has survived from the fourteenth century, indicates that the calls were sounded on just one note, the difference between them being indicated by the rhythm.

Wide use was made of the bugle horn for signaling in battle, both on land and at sea. A corps of thirty buglers took part in the capture of Jerusalem by the Crusaders, and Froissart describes how, in the fourteenth century, squires blew great bugle horns during a battle of the Hundred Years War between the English and the French.[1] The horn tended to be worn as a token of high command, and blown by a commander-in-chief as his personal signal. If he were cut off by the enemy he would blow his horn to rally his bodyguards to his aid. Just in case they did not arrive in time, a medieval horn called an "Oliphant," was usually made so massive that it could be used as a weapon. Count Roland, the great hero of French romances, was cut off by the Saracens as he was leading the rearguard of the army of Charlemagne through the passes of the Pyrenees back to France. In vain he blew his horn as a signal to the Emperor to come to his aid. When at last Charlemagne

1. Encyclopaedia Britannica, eleventh ed., s.v. Horn.

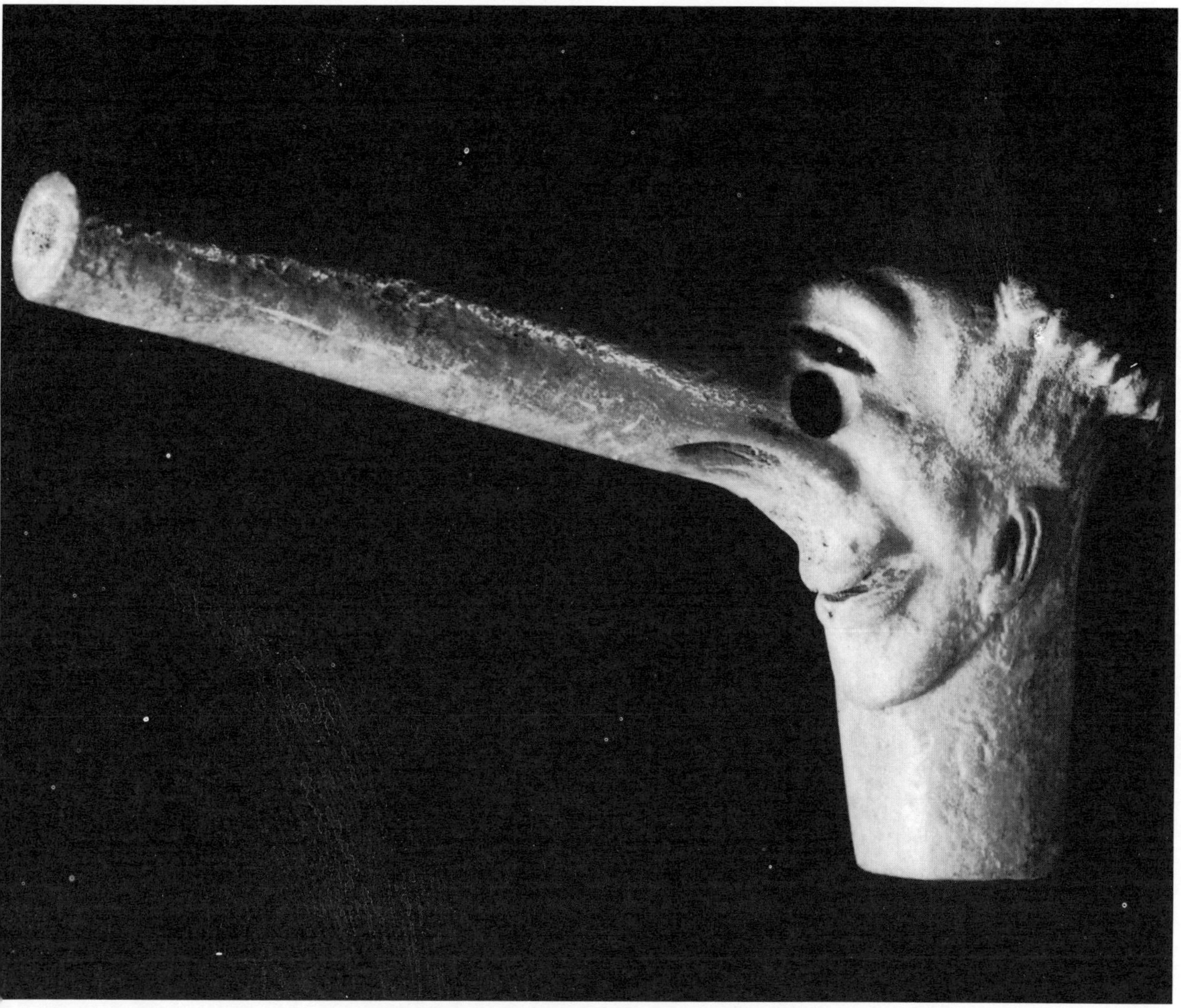

Horn walking stick handle of the fourteenth or fifteenth century, found in Westminster. This handle, made from the tine of an antler, may have belonged to a walking stick carried by one of the many pilgrims to the Shrine of St. Edmund the Confessor in Westminster Abbey. Many pilgrim relics have been found in London. *Courtesy London Museum, Kensington Palace, London, England.*

did hear the note of the horn, it was Roland's death call, he had blown it as a farewell to his friends. When, too late, help arrived, the relief force found Roland dead, lying beside a Saracen who had crept out of the heaps of slain to seize the Count's sword "Durendal." The dying Roland smashed his head in, helmet and all, exclaiming when he had done so. "My oliphant is broken at the mouthpiece, the crystal and gold have fallen from it."

The rich ornaments which covered horns, such as that of Roland, may explain why there are so few medieval horns left. Only

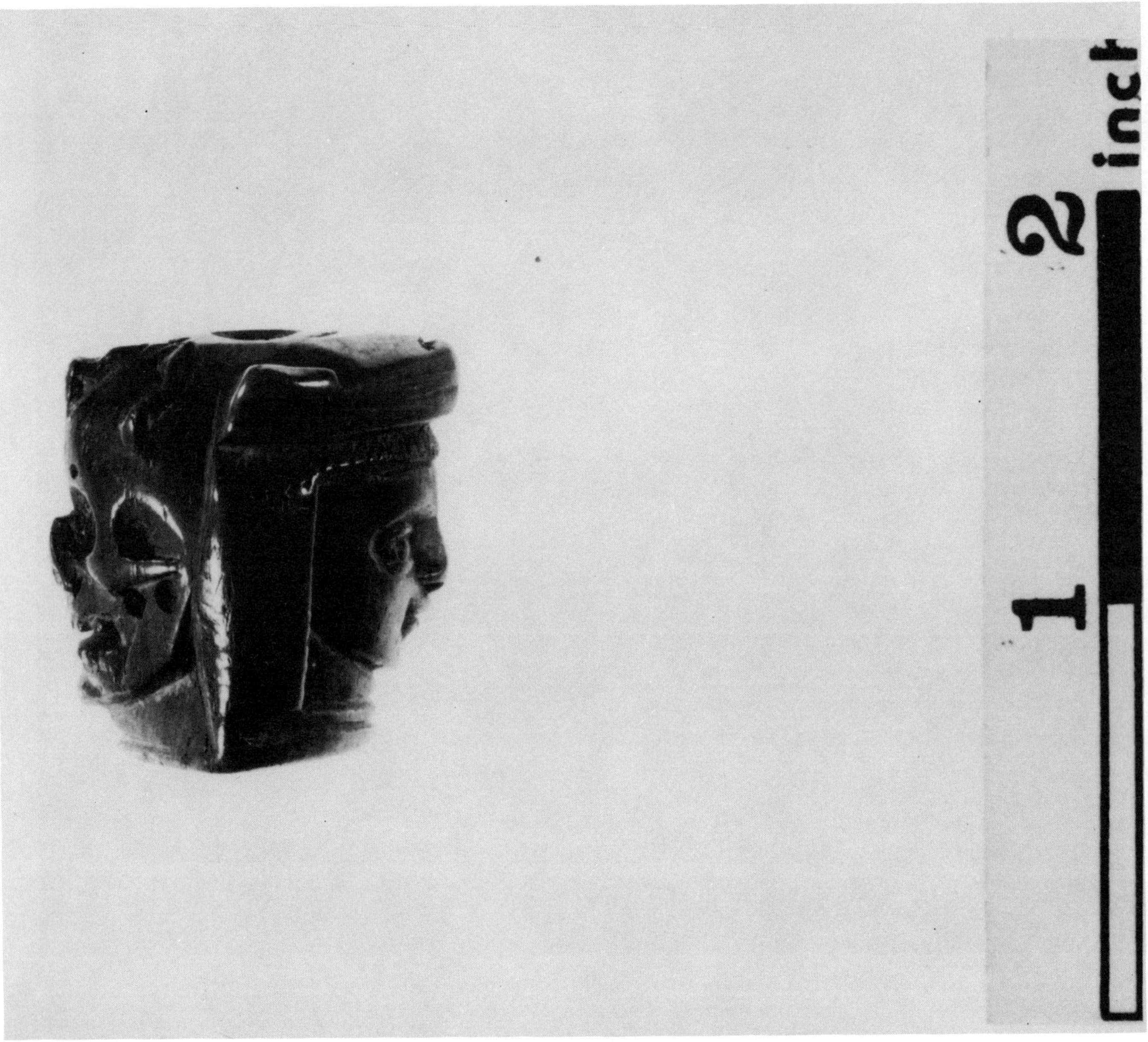

Medieval rosary bead, of bone dyed green, showing the familiar combination of the heads of Death and The Maiden. ***Courtesy London Museum, Kensington Palace, London, England.***

the plain ivory horns which relied on their carved ornament for decoration, have survived in any quantity. Decorated horn bugles were broken up for their ornaments.

Before the heroic era of the Middle Ages had passed away, horn had become associated with another object carried to the battlefield, the crossbow. The crossbow was a Composite Bow in miniature, attached to a wooden staff and pulled back by means of a bowstring levered up to a catch by a "hind's foot." A touch on the trigger released the catch, sending a heavy metal tipped bolt forward with such force that it could transfix a bronze statue and then go on to bury itself in the stone wall of a city. Like the composite bow, the

The Annunciation, diptych in bone mounted on horn, in a frame of silver parcel gilt. Italian, last quarter of the fifteenth century. *Courtesy Victoria and Albert Museum, London, England.*

crossbow was made from a sandwich of different materials. Curators and collectors are understandingly unwilling to sacrifice their treasures, and so far as I know only one crossbow has been dissected. It was made from whalebone, wood, glue, bark and sinew, with horn ends. Horn must have been very necessary for the crossbow, because St. Louis, King of France (who had been saved from the Saracens by a guard of Genoese crossbowmen) sent his trusted engineer, Jean I'Ermin, on what must have been a very dangerous journey through Saracen-occupied territory to Damascus to buy the horn and glue necessary for making crossbows.

The parts of cut up horns not used up as ends for the bow must have represented a waste in the eyes of the craftsman who made them. Perhaps he looked round for new ways of using up this horn. One method of using up horn which quickly suggested itself was to make horn panels with which to line the stock of the crossbow. This was originally made of wood. If left untreated, it could warp, which would mean that the crossbow could not shoot straight or it could be riddled by boring insects, so that it fell to bits, perhaps at a crucial moment, when it was being fired for instance. So horn panels protected the sides and butt of the crossbow staff, while other crossbows, which were not cased completely in horn, had some horn inlay decoration let into the wood. Thus was born the long association of horn and bone first with crossbows, then firearms. Not many of these early crossbows have survived, but a magnificent example is preserved in the Wallace Collection of London, England. It dates from the fifteenth century, and is covered entirely in panels of stag's horn carved into relief. It bears the arms of the family of Fels-

German fifteenth-century coffer with pierced bone panels, depicting knights tilting with men and animals. *Courtesy Victoria and Albert Museum, London, England.*

Detail from the twelfth or thirteenth century. South Italian bone box showing Christ between the Virgin and St. John the Baptist. *Courtesy Victoria and Albert Museum, London, England.*

Detail from the twelfth or thirteenth century. South Italian bone box showing St. Stephen, St. Mark, St. Jude, St. Matthew, St. James the Less, St. Simon, St. Mathias and St. Luke. *Courtesy Victoria and Albert Museum, London, Engand.*

Walnut box of Italian workmanship dating from the twelfth or thirteenth century, covered with bone plaques depicting half-length figures of Christ, the Virgin, the Apostles, and Saints. The carving shows classical and Coptic influences. *Courtesy Victoria and Albert Museum, London, England.*

Colonna of the Tyrol as carried between 1450 and 1470. As if to emphasize the fact that, when firearms arrived, it would be crossbow makers who decorated them, the Fels-Colonna crossbow is ornamented with several types of decoration, all of which are later to appear on decorated firearms. They include erotic scenes, religious themes, pictures of the hunt, people in contemporary costume, knights and heraldic decoration.

The crossbow makers kept their trade secrets a very dark mystery indeed. King René of Anjou, writing in the fifteenth century, explained to his correspondent that he has been quite unable to find out how a crossbow which he is sending him has been manufactured. He has bought it from the Saracen craftsmen of Barcelona, and they are not disposed to talk about their work methods. Other craftsmen apparently put about the rumor that their crossbows were effective because they were made from the *phalli* of elephants.

The secrecy of crossbow makers finds its counterpart in that of other bone and horn workers of the period. Monastic writers are just as chary of giving information about the techniques employed by monastic craftsmen as a modern Carthusian or Benedictine Abbot would be of revealing the secret of Chartreuse or Benedictine, and for the same reason. Monastic craftsmen brought wealth into the monastery, and if lay craftsmen or workmen in other monasteries could copy their methods then the monastery would lose some of its revenue. A medieval manuscript written in the latter half of the twelfth century by Reginald of Durham *The Little Book Of the Wonderful Virtues of the Blessed Cuthbert,* describes how a hunted stag took refuge in the porch of a church in Lothian dedicated to

Saint Cuthbert. The Saint (who loved animals but hated women) drove away the hounds, but the hunters, furious at being robbed of their prey, killed the stag. Hearing of the death of the stag the monastic craftsman (*artificiosus minister*) went off to cut up its bones and horns as raw material. He intended to make from them combs, chessboards and chessmen, dice, and similar objects. However, when he tried to cut off one of the antlers, it spouted blood, and he was forced to declare that the Saint had worked yet another miracle. It is noteworthy that none of the objects which the *artificiosus minister* intended to make were likely to be used by the monks themselves. Their heads were shaved, so they did not require combs, while monastic establishments frowned on time-wasting secular games such as chess, much less gambling with dice. So the *artificiosus minister* obviously intended to sell these objects to laymen and put the money into the monastic budget. If he encouraged competitors he was obviously defrauding his own monastery.

A writer called Theophilus produced a manuscript called *About Different Kinds Of Crafts,* during the early middle ages. The book itself professes to be a handbook on how to make all kinds of art objects. Almost all students of the arts have accepted Theophilus on the strength of his own self praise, and have hailed him as the writer who fills the great gap in our knowledge of medieval craftsmanship by telling us how objects were actually made. Only one commentator, who wrote some fifty years ago, dared to be heretical enough to suggest that Theophilus had merely compiled his information from other books, he knew nothing about craftsmanship himself. I should like to side with this commentator and suggest that when Theophilus tells us how objects are made, he does not speak from practical knowledge.

Let us notice at the start that Theophilus does not describe himself as a craftsman. In his first sentence he tells us that he is a priest and a monk. Well, he ought to know what his profession was, and if he were a priest, why should he have wanted to be a craftsman as well? He would have been of much more use to his monastery by saying masses, of which many were required to commemorate founders and benefactors, than by working in a studio. If he wanted to make money for his monastery he would still be able to make much more money by saying masses than he would ever earn as a craftsman. Even if he were a craftsman, why should he describe his secrets to the whole world, in what a recent editor has admitted was the fluent correct Latin of the literary man? The same editor felt that he was not merely a craftsman, but a great artist, and a practical worker who knew the efficacy of the methods he recommended because he had tried them for himself. Theophilus does tell us that he "has tried out all the receipts one by one and proved them by my hand and eye." One of the methods which he advocates, and which he claims to have tried out for himself, is softening rock crystal by eviscerating a goat and putting the crystal into the wound until it gets warm, after which it will carve easily. Theophilus obviously was aware that there were a lot of goats about, and that the last thing some readers ever did was to try and find out whether something actually worked or not by trying it out for themselves. For years art historians talked of the beautiful blue of Chinese rugs, so like a robin's egg. Then, this year, Dr. H. A. Lorentz went to have a look at a robin's egg, and found that it was white.

I tried one of the "great artist's" receipts for myself. "If you want to carve bone, first shape a tablet of bone to the size you want, put chalk on it, and draw on it with a piece of lead the images you want. Then outline them with a thin burin so that they show up." Although I knew that this receipt would not work I did rub chalk onto a piece of cut bone, and tried to draw a pattern on it. As bone is white, there is no need to whiten it, and as I expected, the lead removed the chalk completely, leaving no line on the bone. Further handling, such as would be necessary to cut in an outline, removed all traces of the chalk. What gives away Theophilus as a literary compiler without practical workshop knowledge is his recommendation of a piece of lead for marking out bone, because a lead pencil was used to mark out the

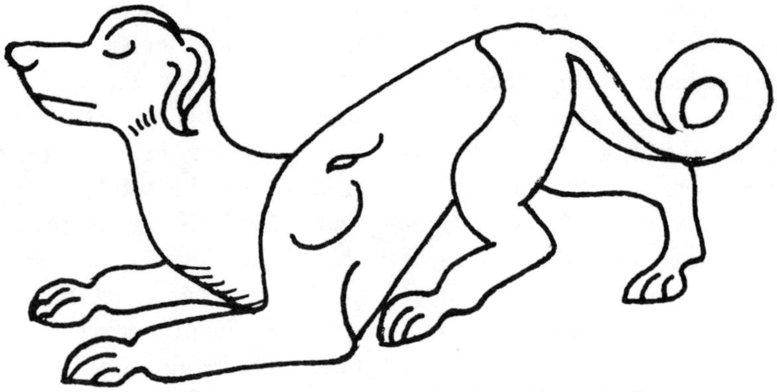

Greyhound from a carved and painted bone coffer made in Moorish Spain in the thirteenth century by Mohammed ben Assarach.

lines of a parchment manuscript, including, probably, the manuscript on which Theophilus wrote. Although lead would not mark chalk on top of bone, it would mark parchment. So much for Theophilus.

A much better guide to the bone carving of the later middle ages than this self-styled expert are the carvings themselves. There is a wealth of small, delightful objects, all of them anonymous, which include bone rosary beads, carved with the usual medieval two heads looking away from one another, chessmen and draughtsmen, pins, and a wonderfully perky face carved on a horn antler, which was intended as the head of a walking stick, and which may have been carved by some pilgrim to pass the leisure moments of his journey.

7

CARVERS TO KINGS

The Embriachi

THE most unaffected compliment which you can pay to a work of art is to steal it. This supreme expression of appreciation has occurred, again and again throughout history, to the works of the most famous carvers of bone of the Renaissance, the Embriachi. Perhaps the most dramatic occasion was in 1782. Benedetto Tordovo, a Carthusian monk at the *Certosa* or Carthusian monastery of Pavia, in Italy, left the monastery when it passed into the hands of a rival order, the Cistercians. So far, so good, but he also took with him the coffers made by the Embriachi of Florence for Gian Galleazzo Visconti, ruler of Milan in the late fourteenth century. Gian Galleazzo had ordered them for his consort, and after the deaths of the royal pair they passed into the possession of the Certosa, and eventually, as has been seen, into the hands of Benedetto Tordovo.

In order to conceal his theft, the ex-monk took some of the coffers to bits. He had some of the bone reliefs they contained assembled with new marquetry work, while he pawned others. When Napoleon was about to be crowned as King of Italy he thought about buying one of the pieces, a cabinet which was worth 8000 lira, as a present for the Empress Josephine. With the reversal of Napoleon's fortunes many of the art treasures of Europe passed into the hands of his victors, who were the only people left with any money, and most of these masterpieces of Italian Renaissance carving found their way to London.

The Embriachi were not merely carvers to princes, they were also princes who had become carvers. In the middle ages they had been a very important noble family in Genoa, founded by a certain Guglielmo, who was a patrician of the city and a military engineer around the year 1070. Military engineers of the time had to be conversant with the working of crossbows, which were largely made from horn and bone, and which were just beginning to appear as an important weapon. This may mark the first association of the Embriachi family with these materials. In 1109 a Genoese fleet sailed into Tripoli, part of the Kingdom of Jerusalem, and helped the crusaders garrisoning the city to repel a great attack by the Saracens. In recognition of their services, the Embriachi family were enfeoffed with the little town of Gibelet, near to the port.

The Embriachi had already begun to devel-

Embriachi box, fifteenth century. To look down on the lid of the box is to look up at the ceilings of the Alhambra in Granada. There Arab craftsmen produced the same kind of marquetry on a larger scale. *Courtesy Victoria and Albert Museum, London, England.*

Embriachi box, fifteenth century. Note the attractive design (the designs of the boxes seldom duplicate themselves) and the marquetry, probably made up by gluing together an amalgam of small sections. *Courtesy Victoria and Albert Museum, London, England.*

op the international tendencies which were to contribute to their success as a family of artists. Nor were they ever to entirely lose the military side to the family impressed on it by the founding father, Guglielmo, because down to the end of their existence as an artistic clan they were to be associated with the fabrication of luxury trappings for cavalrymen.

From the original Genoan house, two main lines of Embriachi descend, the Florentine and the Venetian branches. Messer Aliotto, a presumed descendant of Guglielmo, had as his son Ser Simone, who was in turn succeeded by Ser Baldassarre, described in the records as "a sculptor," who lived between 1389 and 1409 in Florence, and later in Venice. Baldassarre, his eldest son, a love child, was legitimated in 1389. His daughter, Lisabetta, can be traced in the Florence records and later married Piero Chiarini, a cloth merchant, in Venice in 1393.

The other main branch of the family, the Venetian line, is headed by Messer Manfredi, who had two sons, both ivory carvers. The elder was Ser Giovanni, a citizen of Venice, who died in 1433. The younger was Ser Antonio, who also inhabited Venice, and died there in 1431. Ser Giovanni apparently had one son, Ser Niccolo, who was living in Venice around 1412. Ser Antonio had three: Geronimo, an artist who flourished in Venice around 1412, Domenico, also living in Venice at the same time, and Lorenzo, born in Venice in 1409, who moved to Florence and died there in 1483, being buried in the church of Santa Maria Novella.

In between the two branches of the family is Ser Andrea degli Umbriachi, working in Venice as an artist in 1450. He cannot be connected for certain with any of the other members of the family.

This short sketch does not reveal the full ramifications of the Embriachi family, which reached not merely to other Italian towns such as Florence, Modena, and Reggio (where a school of bone carving continued to exist till the end of the eighteenth century) but further afield, to Budapest, Hungary.

If God is on the side of the big battalions He was certainly on the side of the Embriachi. There were so many of them that they probably had representatives in most of the important European cities, including Prague, where Good King Wenceslas was a great admirer and collector of the Embriachi saddles. The best known of the family, such as Baldassarre, were obviously important people with all the right connections. The family had a finger in the ivory carving craft, and part of their success may have lain in the fact that they were able to provide, in a cheaper material, the kind of art products being made by the French ivory carvers. The coffers, combs, and mirror-backs turned out by the Embriachi were completely different in style from those made by the Paris ivory carvers, but they seem to have been aimed at the same market—noble ladies whose mothers were getting together a trousseau for them. Whether the saving in cost produced by working in bone, which could be picked up on the streets, instead of ivory, which had to come all the way from Senegal, and which was an expensive commodity, even in its native Africa, was ever passed on to the customer is a different matter. The Embriachi are always spoken of as excellent men of business and supple Florentines.

There is something very romantic about many of the bridal gifts at which the Embriachi labored for the high born ladies whose dressing tables they were to adorn, such as the coffers presented by Gian Galleazzo to his wife, Caterina. Although Gian had massacred her father and brothers, Caterina seems to have loved him, and he seems to have loved her, in spite of the fact that, according to Renaissance ideas, her duty lay in revenging her kin.

Chests, mirrors, combs, and hairpins all featured in the trousseau presents given to brides, but the most important items seem to have been the jewel cases, which often bear the joint coats of arms of bride and groom. The high workmanship of these little boxes made them treasured family heirlooms. The same high quality of craftsmanship made them suitable reliquaries for enclosing holy relics in churches. Just such a reliquary is mentioned in the expenses of the Carthusian monastery of Pavia. The Prior admits to still owing the

Embriachi box, fifteenth century. This fine example shows the ever-changing design of the box itself: the Gothic architectural decor, remains of painting at the bottom of the carved panels, the stylized mushroom trees, and the foreshortened cow. *Courtesy Victoria and Albert Museum, London, England.*

Embriachi box with the story of Jason. Note the delightfully original shape of the box, the very narrow sections of bone used for the carvings, and the brilliant *alla certosina* marquetry. *Courtesy Victoria and Albert Museum, London, England.*

final payment due to Francesco de Masis of Florence for a carved tablet (part of the famous carved altar of La Certosa, the Carthusian church) and two *coafani,* or boxes of bone and ivory. The Prior agreed to pay the installment by the following Easter. It has been argued that the Prior must have wanted these coffers for his own use, not for that of the church, because they were sculptured with very secular subjects. Worldly imagery did occur on reliquaries, however, such as the Franks Casket. Reliquaries, after all, were not on display to the public, but were kept in the treasury of the church. The frames for the mirrors were octagonal, and had a pointed finial at the top. Like the jewel boxes, they formed a regular item in a bride's trousseau, as did combs and lantern holders. Comb makers in Italy belonged to their individual guild, with which the Embriachi may have been affiliated. Some of the products of the family seem to have been the speciality of localities. Bone spurs were made in Reggio, for example, while combs and lantern holders were very much a product of northeastern Italy.

The presents for trousseaus seem to have been all custom built, at the request of individual patrons, who often stipulated about the carving or painting of their arms on the finished article. By contrast, the portable altars which the Embriachi made seem to have been created as a speculation in the hope that they would find a patron. Although, strictly speaking, any altar ought to be made from stone, bone seems to have been equated with stone for theological purposes, and, as has been noticed already, whalebone had been popular for altars during the Romanesque period. The Embriachi also made folding bone triptychs which could be carried about on journeys.

Patrons, whether ladies, churchmen, or knights, seem to have taken the greatest pride in their bone carvings, and probably prefered them to the walrus tooth or elephant ivory carvings brought to Italy by northern merchants. Unlike ivory, bone carvings were a brilliant white, which did not dull with the passing of time. In spite of the fact that at least two of the family were ivory carvers, bone was so much more the favored substance that it has been described as the national material for carving in Italy during this period.

Lid of the Embriachi Jason Box. Notice the blank shields, ready to be carved with the coats of arms of customers on demand. *Courtesy Victoria and Albert Museum, London, England.*

Lid of Embriachi box with hunting scenes. ***Courtesy Victoria and Albert Museum, London, England.***

It was only rarely that the Embriachi carved ivory at all. Then it took the form of large pieces of work carved from hippopotamus teeth for the *Certosa* in Pavia. Otherwise they preferred their chosen material, the neck and shoulder bones of horses and cattle.

Like the contemporary French ivory carvers, the Embriachi believed in gilding the lily. The sparkling white bone disappeared in a riot of lively color. Relief was underlined by a liberal use of gilt on a red background. Gilding also picked up the contours, while the spaces provided by the background to the carvings, or by the clothes of the figures, were given a richly patterned design of flowers. Other parts of the carving, such as the mouth of a figure, would be touched up in red.

Equally colorful was the marquetry mosiac applied to the boxes and other carvings. They were made up in colored woods, dyed bone and horn, and plain white bone, which provided a sparkling contrast to the dark tints of the surrounding elements in the pattern. The inlay elements are all geometrical, roundels, squares, lozenges, diamonds, and so forth, and they are grouped into composite patterns arranged like stars or circles.

A typical Embriachi box would be six-sided, with sides and lid of bone, stained a brilliant green. A band of bone carving, which would originally have been covered with color and gilding, would run round the edge of the lid. On each side there would be an individual panel of carved bone, surrounded by a frame of marquetry. Each frame would have a different pattern. A band of marquetry decoration would run round the bottom of the box, just above the feet upon which the box rested.

Although no one seems to have commented on the fact before, the Embriachi had imported an entirely new art form into Christian Europe, an art form which was already old in the Muslim East, and which was to continue to have a long life there, so long in fact that for the best description of how the Embriachi actually made their marquetry, we shall have to turn to George C. M. Birdwood, who observed craftsmen in British India carrying out the same kind of work in 1863.

A glance at Embriachi marquetry will show that though parts of it are made up of large and rather crude elements, other parts are composed of very tiny pieces of inlay, arranged symmetrically around a center. These symmetrical patterns repeat identically, again and again, while the larger elements show somewhat more variation among themselves. It would have been an extremely laborious task to have cut every tiny element of the smaller sized designs, and then stick it in place, and we know that the Embriachi did not like long, finicky jobs, on which there was little profit; they preferred quick, mass production methods. On the other hand they could have produced their marquetry, very quickly and cheaply, by making it up in the

Side view of Embriachi box with hunting scenes.
Courtesy Victoria and Albert Museum, London, England.

Embriachi box with hunting scenes, fifteenth century. ***Courtesy Victoria and Albert Museum, London, England.***

same way that inlayers of similar boxes in Bombay did during the nineteenth century. The inlayers, who had learned their craft from Persian artists who had emigrated to Sindh from Shiraz, about 1800, simply prepared rods or strips of inlay material, sandalwood, ebony, brazil wood, ivory, white and stained green, stag horn and *sambur* horn, also stained. These rods were then glued together and bound up tightly till they dried. Sections were then cut across them, and these thin slices, which showed all the different colors and shapes in combination, were then glued onto a wooden base or sunk into an inlay recess. The patterns were made up in three-sided rods, round ones, six-sided ones, three-cornered ones, square, and oblong bordering patterns. This technique, which was to be re-discovered or copied by the marquetry workers who made Tunbridge Ware in England during the eighteenth and nineteenth centuries, enabled a worker to make up a marquetry pattern in a tithe of the time he would have taken to cut each individual piece, much less glue it in place.

The immediate inspiration for marquetry work of this sort must have come from Arab Spain. There what was called *taracea,* a marquetry decoration virtually identical with that employed by the Embriachi, was used to decorate boxes made up of carved ivory panels, the *mimbars* or pulpits of mosques, such as the mosque chapel of the Alcazaba, or citadel, of Marrakus, an Almohavid fortress in Spain, or the ceilings of palaces, such as the Alhambra in Granada.

Ultimately this marquetry work had been derived from the Hellenistic mosaics of Alexandria. Mosaics of this sort had been copied in the Mosque of Cordoba by Al Hakam II, ruler of Cordoba in the ninth century. The Caliph's cabinet makers imitated the stone mosaics in wood, making use of a technique which was practical as well as ornamental, as

Embriachi box, fifteenth century. Though it has an excitingly shaped top, this all-bone box is far from achieving the success of the mixed bone and *alla certosina* examples. *Courtesy Victoria and Albert Museum, London, England.*

doors and furniture made from many small pieces of wood, rather than several large ones, would be much less likely to split and warp in the dry hot climate of Spain. From Spain the art passed to Egypt, and Cairene marquetry from the ninth century is still in existence.

It was a far cry from the marquetry of Moorish Spain to that of the Embriachi. Moorish marquetry was carried out in the richest materials available, ivory, ebony, citron wood, *bakam,* aloes, sandalwood, even gold and silver. The richness of the materials used was matched in the painstaking nature of the workmanship. The marquetry for the *mimbar* or pulpit ordered by Hakam II for the mosque at Cordoba cost 35,705 dinars and took five years to complete, while the travel writer al Idrisi cites another *mimbar* which took seven years to finish.

The Embriachi would be hardly likely to have undertaken an order which took seven years to complete. There would have been no profit in it. Part of their success lay in the speedy, mass-production methods which they employed. Even the shape of their raw material, bone helped to achieve standardization, and therefore efficiency, in their work methods. Bone does not offer a wide surface upon which to carve, such as a slab of ivory, but rather a fairly narrow convex plaque. These plaques were lined up on a wooden core, such as a box, or whatever else was being made, and glued in place. The decorative motifs carved on one plaque usually did not overlap onto the others, they were confined to just one piece of bone. The top of a plaque was almost always decorated with a grotesque landscape of rocks and trees, which look rather like mushrooms. The regularity in which these trees were carved shows that the inspiration for tree designs had originally come from one single source. It was a great benefit to a workman to carve only one kind of tree. He did not have to wonder about what he was to carve, or waste time looking round for a model. He had carved so many mushroom trees that he could make them in his sleep if need be, so he could get through the day's task that much more quickly.

It was not just trees and other parts of the background which came in standardized shapes and sizes. The figures in the Embriachi carvings also show a strong family likeness to one another, a feature which has helped art historians very much in tracking down the far scattered Embriachi pieces. In fact, fidelity to a model, patience, and accuracy were much

Fifteenth-century bone box, partly set with *alla certosina* marquetry, and partly with pierced panels depicting "Wodehouses," or wild men, a common medieval theme. *Courtesy Victoria and Albert Museum, London, England.*

more important to an Embriachi workman than genius.

The workshop was like a well organized factory. Many of the pieces were not composed as a whole, but put together from units which happened to be handy. The existence of some of these "ready-made" bone carvings can be seen from the fact that some boxes bear flying angels carrying heraldic shields which have not been carved, but left blank, so that the coat of arms of the patron, whoever he might be, could be added to them later. Another indication that work went forward in putting together units which were already at hand is the way in which the chequerwork of prepared marquetry borders is simply sawn across where they have to join, without any attempt to make a connecting piece.

It has been suggested that the very mechanical nature of this kind of art work made it a preferred task in monasteries, where everything was done to stifle the individual. Marquetry in the Embriachi manner was so popular in Carthusian monasteries in Lombardy that its very name, in Italian (*alla Certosiana*) means "Carthusian."

Of course, in the case of some products, such as the bone saddles which were made at the end of the fifteenth century, mass production might be said to be a necessity. Many hands would be needed to carve and set in place the bone plaques required by just one saddle.

One can almost hear Baldassarre, or some other member of the family, exclaiming, "Let's use these bits up," or "Put those plaques in here, there's just room for them." The result has been to create compositions in which apparently unrelated figures stand side by side, figures whom no legend that the puzzled art historians can think of can connect.

How can works of art so standardized and regimented have any appeal at all? The charm of Embriachi art lies, I suspect, in its unexpected qualities. The awkward form of a bone plaque forced the artist to compress his figures into it, giving them a grotesque beauty, like a Chinese jade carving, forced into the confines of a natural pebble. There is nothing medieval about a cow, so foreshortened by the width of the bone plaque as to be virtually square. Just because it is so unlike the rest of medieval and Renaissance art, it makes an instant appeal. This appeal seems to have been felt by patrons, contemporary with the Embriachi, who had very diverse tastes in art. They were bought both by people wholly medieval in outlook, like the Duc de Berri, and men wholly of the Renaissance, such as Gian Galleazzo Visconti.

Aware that they had admirers in both camps, the Embriachi seem to have tried to woo both sets of patrons at the same time by employing themes drawn alternately from the medieval and the Renaissance world. Thus they represented medieval themes such as the Virtues, the Scholastic Circle, Courtly Love, Patient Griselda, Mattabruna, and others, together with many religious motifs, such as the figures of the saints. To tempt the humanist, on the other hand, they deployed themes such as the stories of Jason, Paris, Pyramus and Thisbe, Hero and Leander, and Theseus.

This two-fold inspiration was accompanied by the family tradition of internationalism. The Embriachi were not merely stretched right across Europe, they also employed many non-Italian workmen, Germans attracted south of the Brenner by the fame of their handicraft, and French ivory carvers.

None of their products are so international as the saddles, or saddlebows, covered with bone plaques painted green, red, and blue, which were so much admired by warriors of the time. Decorative motifs on these saddles include a hand emerging from a sleeve, initials in a wreath of radiance, fluttering ribbons, ladies wearing crowns and kneeling as though imploring deliverance by some noble knight, and Gothic towers. These themes have been derived from contemporary Italian majolica, just as the doors of the Baptistery at Florence served as a design manual for the Embriachi artists of that city, but they are accompanied by legends often northern in inspiration. Sometimes these legends are even carved in German, rather than Italian or Latin. "I hope for the best, God help me in the name of St. George." "Remember, and be steadfast."

The Embriachi may have felt that they

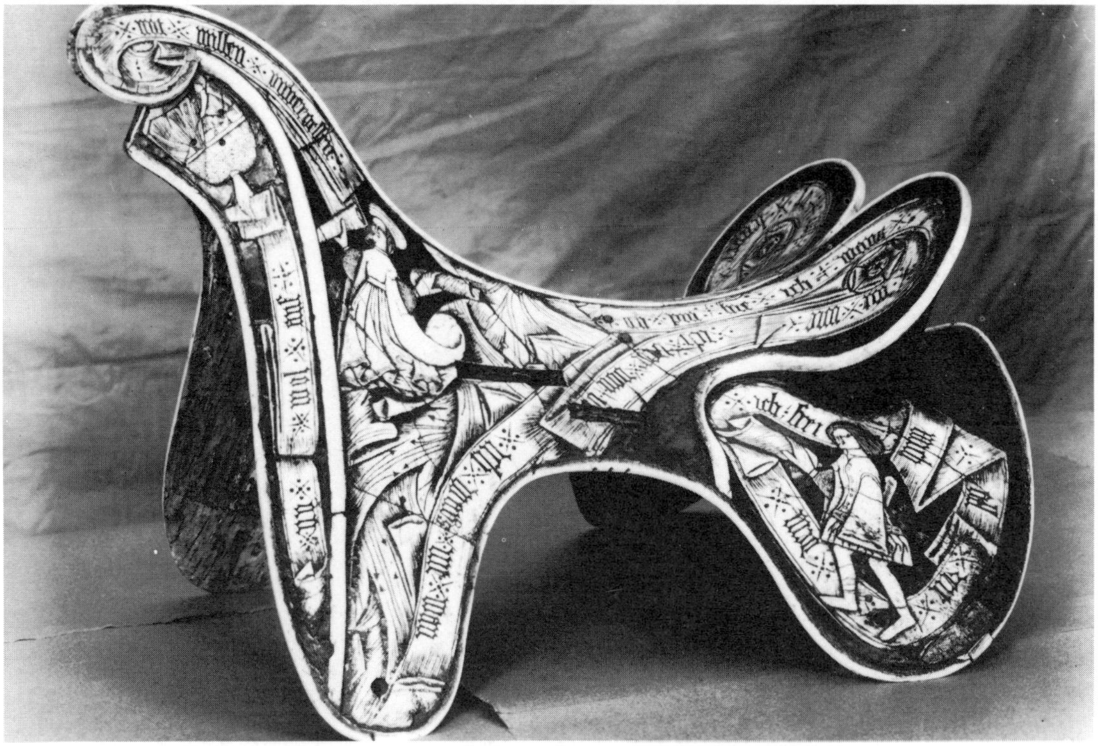

Fifteenth-century saddle made of wood, faced with plaques of stag's horn incised and partly stained red, green, and black. It is carved with the figures of two lovers who exchange a dialogue in which they promise never to forget one another, no matter how widely they may be separated. The German inscription and Gothic figures are very much in the style of the Embriachi. *Courtesy Wallace Collection, London, England.*

Saddle bow of the same saddle. *Courtesy Wallace Collection, London, England.*

must put something on the saddles which would appeal directly to their customers—and the flame of chivalry, still burning bright in the lands of the Emperor, had completely died in the country of the *condottieri.* One Albert of Sienna, always called "the madman," because of his shrewd commonsense, was asked to take part in a forthcoming campaign. "Twenty five *scudi* will be paid you in compensation if your horse gets killed," he was told. "And how much compensation will you pay if I get killed?" asked Albert. When told that the compensation only applied to horses, not their riders, he replied. "Good, in that case I'll send my horse and stay at home myself."[1]

No final judgement on the Embriachi ought to ignore what was probably their greatest service to the art of marquetry. By creating coffers in intriguing and very unusual shapes they broke away finally from the heavy, sarcophagus-like caskets which, in the shape of the Andalusian boxes of marquetry and ivory or bone, had been their inspiration. Light and delicate, an Embriachi box is like a little renaissance *tempietto* with an architectural grace all its own. Like the Renaissance itself it is determined to combine the best of everything, the spirit of chivalry and of religion, the exotic arts of the Muslim world together with the newly discovered world of Greece and Rome. All is *virtu;* the elegant outline, the bold carving, and the delicate marquetry in glowing colors, all combine to charm.

1. This story, in its original form, appeared in Franco Sachetti, *Novelle,* Vol. 1 (Florence: Filippo Umberti, 1724), p. 22.

8

PLAYTHINGS FOR PRINCES

Renaissance Decorated Gun Stocks

LIKE the Stone Age, the Renaissance was an era noted for the application of fine bone and horn carving to weaponry, but whereas the earlier period had seen the fashioning of every conceivable weapon from bone, the Renaissance confined its use to two principal items, the gunstock and the powder flask. It is not difficult to see why the ornamentation of guns should have reached its apogee at this period. It was the age of the individual, and the gun is essentially an individual weapon. The medieval sportsman had required a pack of hounds to pin down his game, or beaters to drive it within range of his crossbow. The invention of the wheel lock arquebus in 1517 made it possible for the lone sportsman to walk abroad in search of birds or chamois.

Benvenuto Cellini, the famous Florentine goldsmith who personified many of the virtues, and all the vices, of the Renaissance, was never happier than when walking amid the ruins of the Forum, or the Appian way at Rome, shooting pigeons, and chaffering with the tillers of the vineyards for the antique gems and coins which they had dug up during their labors. The only relief from the monotony of Benvenuto's accounts of his success with Art, Woman, and Homicide is when he breaks off to describe his achievements as a sportsman with his "wonderful little gun," which he called "Broccardo." With it he could nick a farthing, or decapitate a wood pigeon, or so he says, and he may indeed have been a good shot with an arquebus, for it was with this weapon that he killed the Postmaster of Sienna, and perhaps even, as he claims, shot the greatest soldier in Europe, the Constable de Bourbon, as he was leading his men to the storming of the Castello Santangelo. Here was another reason why men of the Renaissance became obsessed with guns. With a gun in his hand a goldsmith like Benvenuto, untrained in any of the martial arts, became the equal of the best professional soldiers in Europe. "Powder and ball, will level all," as one eighteenth-century American inscribed on his powder horn. Benvenuto had learned this lesson on seeing his brother, armed only with a sword, shot down by an arquebusier in a street brawl.

In the short time it took Benvenuto to grow from boyhood to manhood the gun had ceased to be just a plain serviceable weapon and became a collector's item, acquired much more because of its decoration and ornament, and the ingenuity of its mechanism than for its potentialities for bringing down game.

The change can be seen in just two of the guns which Benvenuto himself owned. The first, which he made himself, was obviously just a plain, serviceable, fowling piece, even if it did have a highly polished barrel. The second was a present from Duke Alessandro de Medici of Florence. Benvenuto describes how he was given the arquebus.

"We were in the duke's cabinet while this talk was going on, and his grace was busy looking at a magnificent little gun which had been sent him from Germany. Noticing that I was looking at the pretty gadget with the utmost interest, he handed it to me, saying he knew how things of this sort pleased me, and that to show that his promises to me had been sincere, I might help myself to any of the arquebuses he had in his armoury, all except this particular one, though there were many just as beautiful, and as good, in the place. I accepted this offer with thanks, and seeing my eyes wandering round in search of an arquebus, he told his Master of the Cabinet, a certain Pretino da Lucca, to allow me to carry off whichever arquebus I pleased. Then, after saluting me politely, he left. I stayed to make choice of the best and most beautiful arquebus which I ever had in my life, and carried it home with me."[1]

In fact the ornamented gun had become an object of display, and of princely munificence, intended to be given away as a royal present to an important personage. As late as the opening years of the nineteenth century this tradition was still being carried on. Napoleon would order a fowling piece, or a pair of pistols, of so many thousand francs worth, from the imperial armories, and send it as a present to a foreign head of state. The price of the gun would of course depend on the amount of workmanship lavished on it. Although by Napoleon's time silver and other metals had become much more prominent in gun decoration than horn and bone, fine guns ornamented with horn inlay continued to be made well into the eighteenth century, and Napoleon owned several of them himself.

Why had the gun, once just a plain and utilitarian tool, become overnight, as it were, a sort of art museum in itself, covered with beautiful horn carving and inlay, and with a chiseled, gilded and damascened barrel? Fine decoration in horn and bone had been applied to crossbows as early as the fifteenth century. It was from the decoration of crossbows that the decoration of guns obviously originated. Both would be looked after by the same official, in the case of Henry VIII of England, Giles Churchill, the Yeoman of the Crossbows.

One reason why fine ornament took some time to appear on guns was that it took some time for royal patrons to accustom themselves to shooting with anything except a crossbow. Typical of this old fashioned attitude among sportsmen was the Emperor Maximilian (1459–1519) who issued edicts preventing peasants hunting with guns. Yet even Maximilian had himself painted hunting chamois with a gun (a perfectly plain and unornamented matchlock). Then, some time between 1493 and 1508, he ordered one of the first sporting rifles ever to be made. This bore decoration; twisting curlicues of horn, and the imperial arms.

Of course there were good reasons why the guns of important persons should start being ornamented. Their armorers would feel that it was not right that they should go about with ordinary guns, just like anyone else. An overall decoration of horn inlay would help to repel the wood-boring insects that would otherwise riddle the stock with holes. Furthermore, if someone like Maximilian persisted in going out shooting with a gun exactly like all those carried by his soldiers, the chances were it would get mixed up with one belonging to someone else. In that case the Emperor might be handed a gun that bore the wrong charge of powder (everyone had his own preference in this respect, Benvenuto Cellini used a charge that weighed a fifth of the ball) or worse still, was unloaded, at some crucial moment in the hunt.

Ornamentation, even simple ornamentation, would prevent one gun being exchanged for

1. Benvenuto Cellini, *Memoirs of Benvenuto Cellini, A Florentine Artist, Written by Himself* (London: Dent, Everyman Edition, 1913) p. 185, 242 and passim for Benvenuto's exploits with his gun.

another. So decoration began to appear, at first in the shape of simple spirals, squares, or roundels, engraved rudely with the figures of monsters, then in the form of elaborate grotesques and interlacing strapwork. The change from penny-plain to twopenny-colored guns can be seen in the armory of Henry VIII. In the early years of his reign his outlay on firearms had been negligible, but by the end of it he had acquired several fine firearms, one of them a gun inlaid with bone.

Many of the epochs of bone carving that we have looked at in this book have been marked by anonymous masterpieces. The artists who inlaid stag's horn ornaments on the stocks and butts of guns are no exception to this rule. One reason for this anonymity may have been that the gun stockers rarely, if ever, came into direct contact with the patron who bought the gun. A gun maker who forged and bored gun barrels, and made the lock mechanisms, would contract out the job of decorating the wooden stock with horn and bone to a specialist craftsman in these materials. If the inlayer carried out other kinds of work, such as making inlaid gaming boards, small cabinets, coffers and writing desks, we are much more likely to know something about him than if he merely made gun stocks. This was because his name would appear in the court records as the recipient of a payment for a particular piece of furniture. Wigullus Elsesser, for example, an Innsbruck craftsman who made a beautiful coffer inlaid with staghorn for Archduke Ferdinand of the Tirol in 1566, has been traced in this way. Often we only know about a gun stocker, not because he was particularly eminent in his profession, but because he was literate and described himself as a "*monsteur d'harquebus*" ("mounter of arquebusses") or "*maistre monteur et graveur de musquets,*" ("master mounter and engraver of muskets") as does Jeremie Belquin, one of the founders of the famous Belkein family of shell engravers, who so signed the records at Utrecht in 1608 and 1617.

J. C. Tornier of Massevaux in Lorraine (the same province from which Jeremie Belquin came) is also comparatively well known, because he signed his beautiful walnut coffers: "Made in Massevaux by Jean Conrad Tornier, arquebus mounter."

On the whole it is unusual to be able to penetrate the disguise of a gun stocker when he signs himself, as he usually does if he signs at all, with a monogram, or his initials. We know that "H. B." stands for Hieronymus Borstorffer, a stockmaker who worked in Mu-

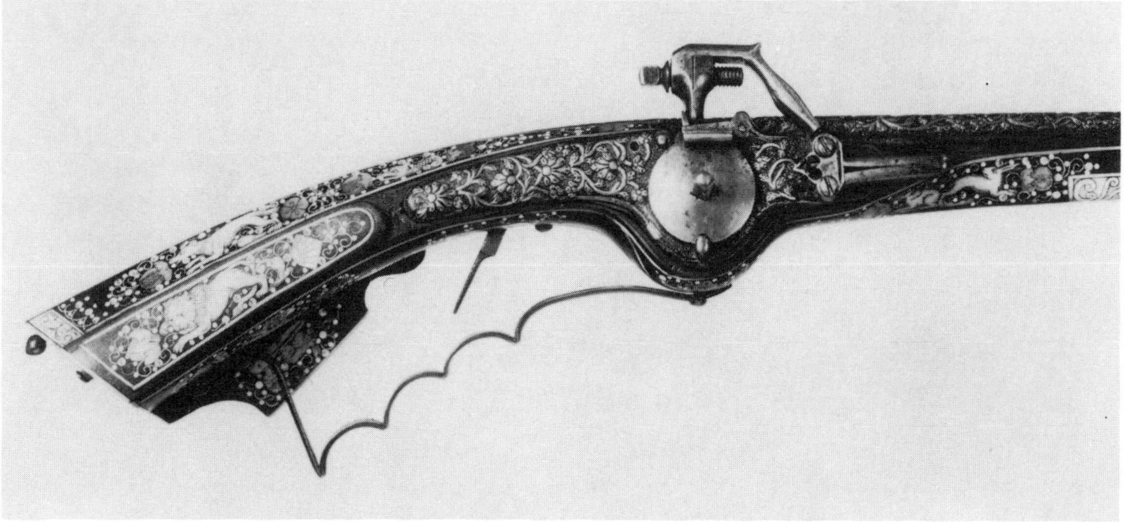

German wheel-lock petronel, made in Silesia about 1630, with stock decorated with inlay in the Tschinke style. *Courtesy Wallace Collection, London, England.*

nich between 1595 and his death in 1637, partly because of his close association with Daniel and Emmanuel Sadeler, Munich gunsmiths to the Electors of Bavaria, but there are many other gun stockers, just as talented, who will forever remain known just by their initials.

The type of gun that was to be decorated, the preference of the gun maker, and the taste and talents of the gun stocker, all helped to determine how the ornamentation was to be carried out. Thus the Tschinkes, Silesian gunsmiths working in the 1630's, preferred a walnut stock inlaid with birds, grotesques and animals in stag's horn, together with circular mother of pearl plaques. The light wheel-lock rifles made in the north of Germany and in the Baltic countries were almost always decorated with a horn carving or engraving of St. George and the Dragon on the cheek piece. Jean Conrad Tornier of Massevaux had a fondness for hunting scenes, and ornaments of fruit and flowers among which birds and animals disport themselves. He took the engraved ornament of Michel le Blon for the inspiration of his inlays, and went on using the same designs right through his career.

The personality of the owner was also reflected in gun decoration. Although the gun stocker never dealt with him directly, he would be informed, by the gun maker, what the patron wanted. If he were a married man, he might have his initials, and his wife's, joined together on the cheek piece of a gun. If he were a bachelor, fond of a broad joke with the pretty peasant girls he met while out hunting, he might want his gun stock embellished with erotic scenes—ornaments which would provide an unspoken provocation to raillery and flirtation. If the owner were an extremely religious person, or someone who realized how frequently guns made in the sixteenth and seventeenth centuries burst and wanted to be looking at something suitable during his last moments, the gun stocker would embellish the gun with scenes of the Crucifixion, images of saints, and so forth.

It is not possible to go through the fine guns which are still in existence and demon-

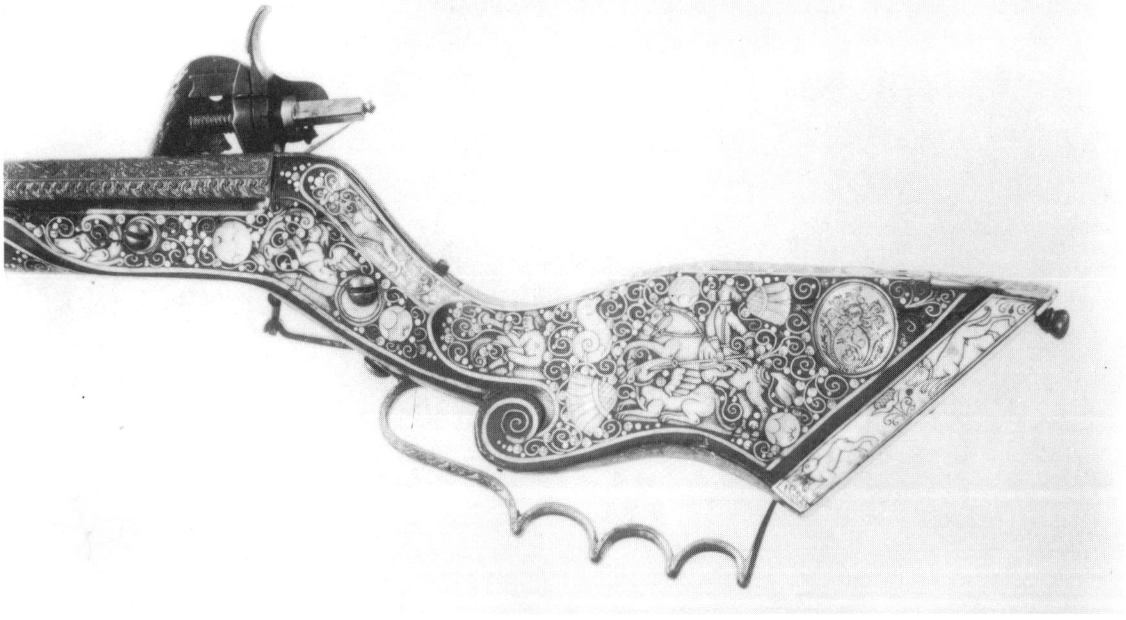

Tschinke wheel-lock, made in Silesia about 1630, with the usual walnut stock favored by the Tschinkes, inlaid with birds, animals and grotesque figures in engraved stag's horn. *Courtesy Wallace Collection, London, England.*

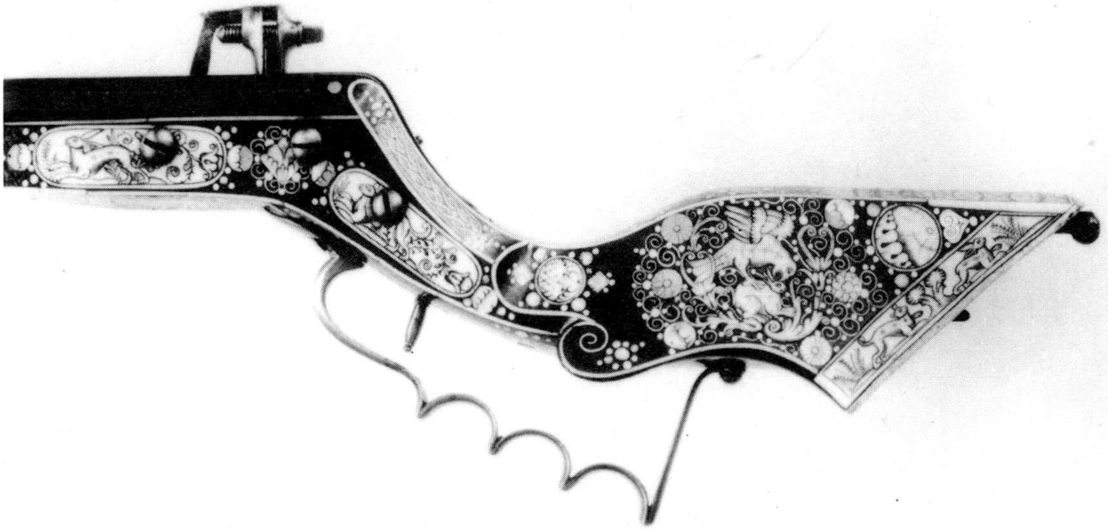

Tschinke wheel-lock rifle, with a walnut stock inlaid with hares and hounds in stag's horn. Silesian, about 1630. *Courtesy Wallace Collection, London, England.*

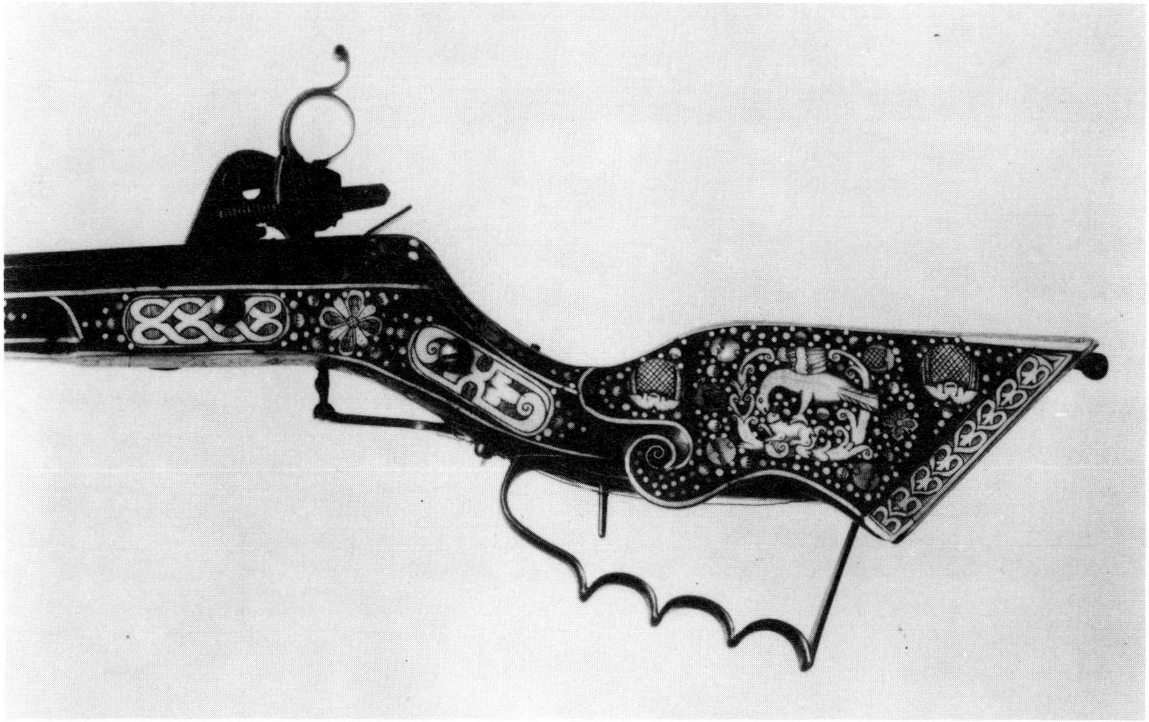

Tschinke wheel-lock rifle, signed "P.K." The stock is inlaid with oval and circular plaques of stag's horn and panels of strapwork. On the butt is a hawk attacking a hare. Silesian, about 1630. *Courtesy Wallace Collection, London, England.*

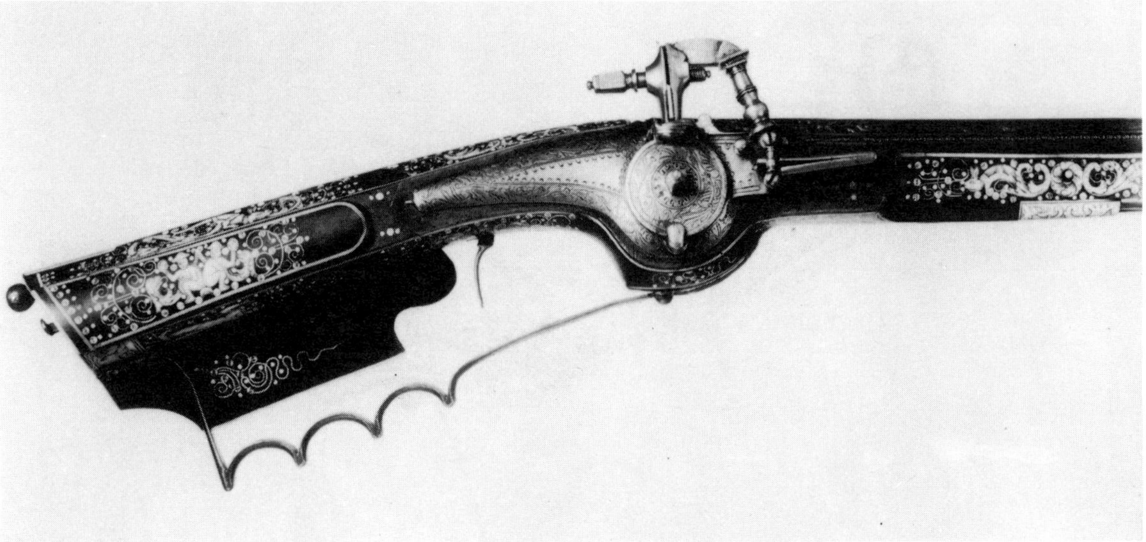

Petronel of about 1630, with a walnut stock inlaid with monsters, coats of arms and terminal figures. *Courtesy Wallace Collection, London, England.*

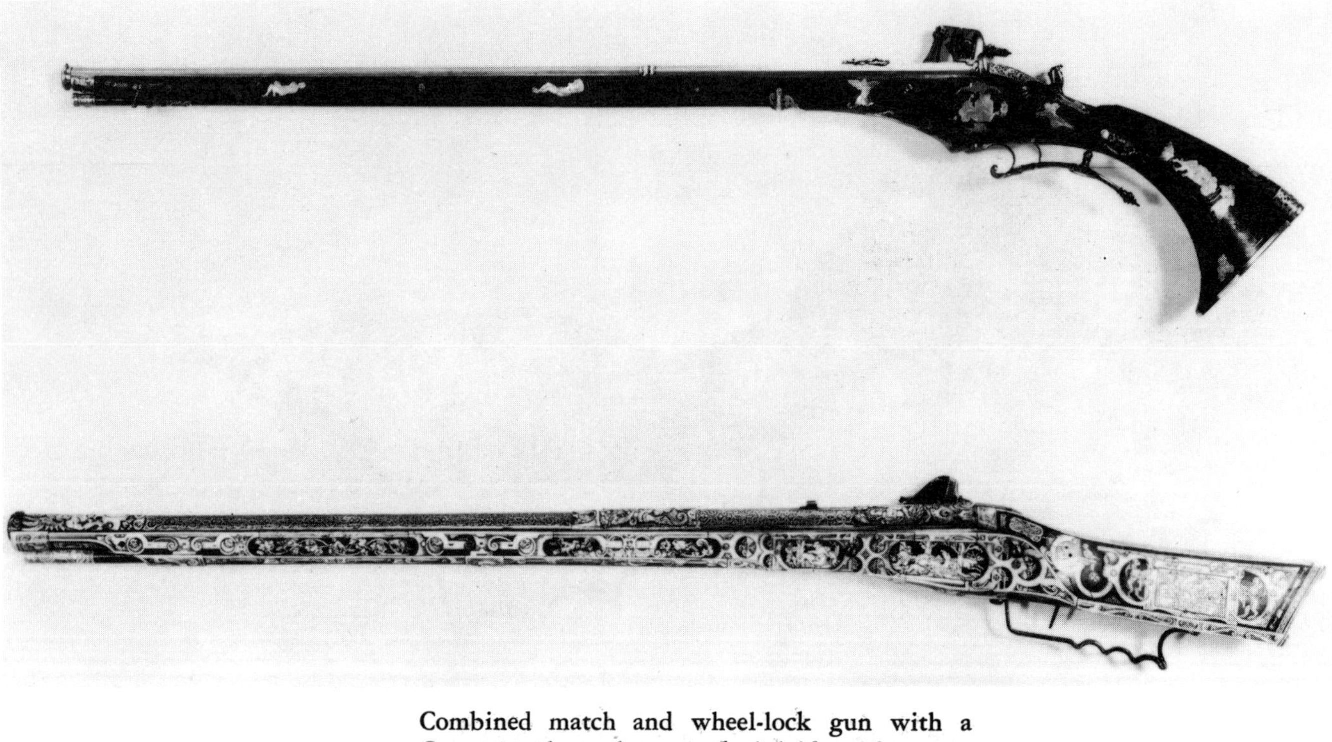

Combined match and wheel-lock gun with a German-style walnut stock inlaid with strapwork animals and foliage in stag's horn. About 1630. *Courtesy Wallace Collection, London, England.*

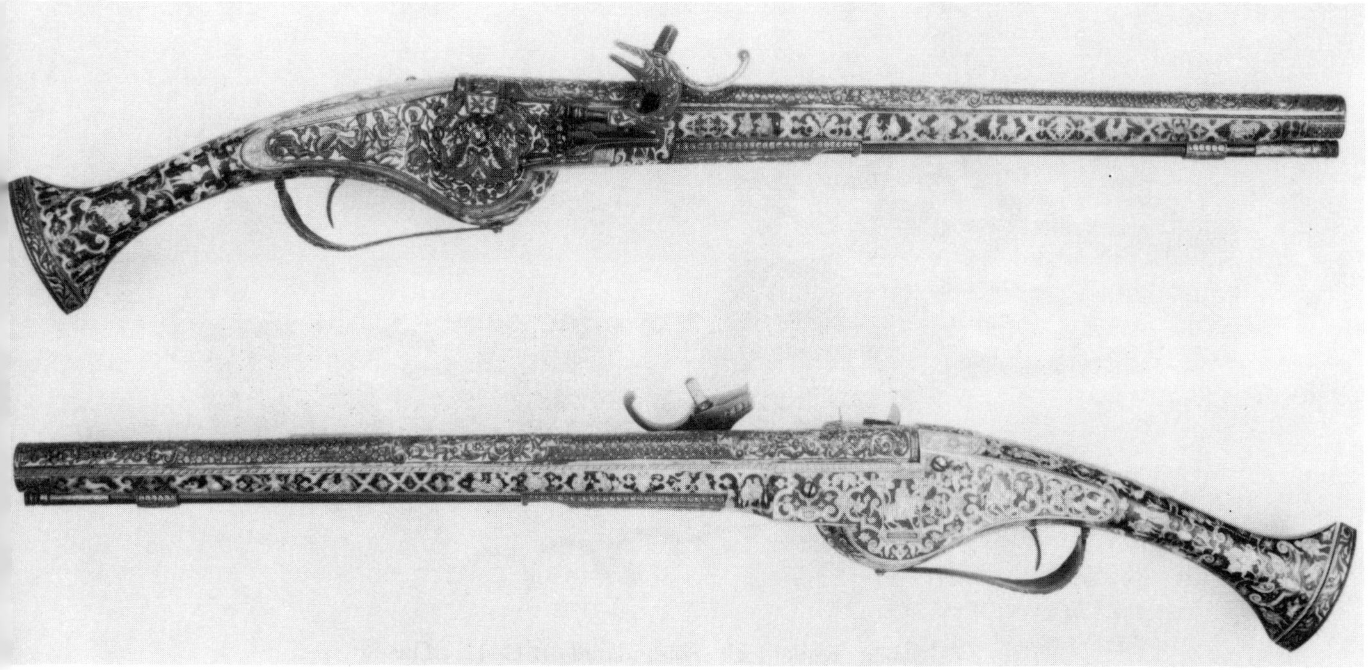

Silesian stocked petronel of about 1630. Decorated in the manner of the Tschinkes, the stock is inlaid with hounds, rabbits, squirrels and grotesques. *Courtesy Wallace Collection, London, England.*

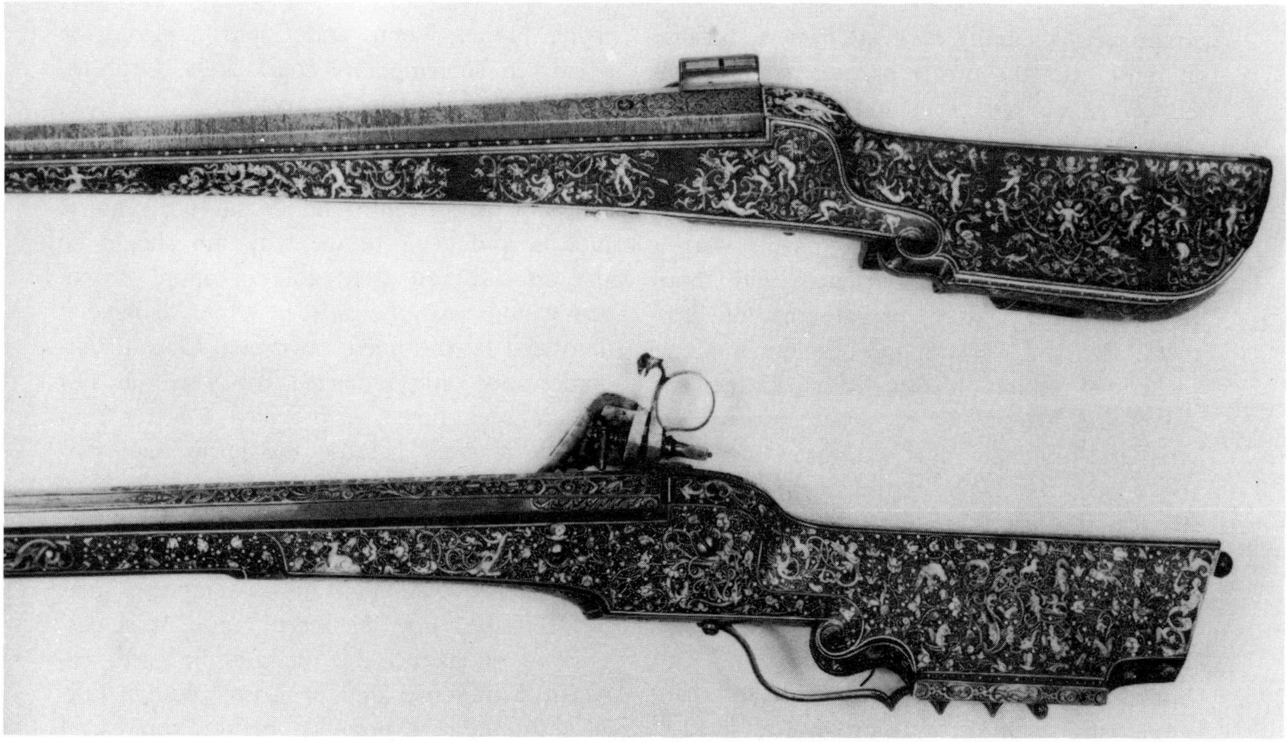

Wheel-lock rifle, with stock inlaid with plaques of stag's horn in the form of deer, hounds, squirrels, human figures and monsters. Blank spaces are filled with scrolls and circular spots of stag's horn. Silesian, about 1620. Bottom, wheel-lock rifle, probably a Saxon, about 1650. Fine interlacing floral scrolls interspersed with birds, squirrels and grotesque terminal figures ornament this walnut stock. *Both courtesy Wallace Collection, London, England.*

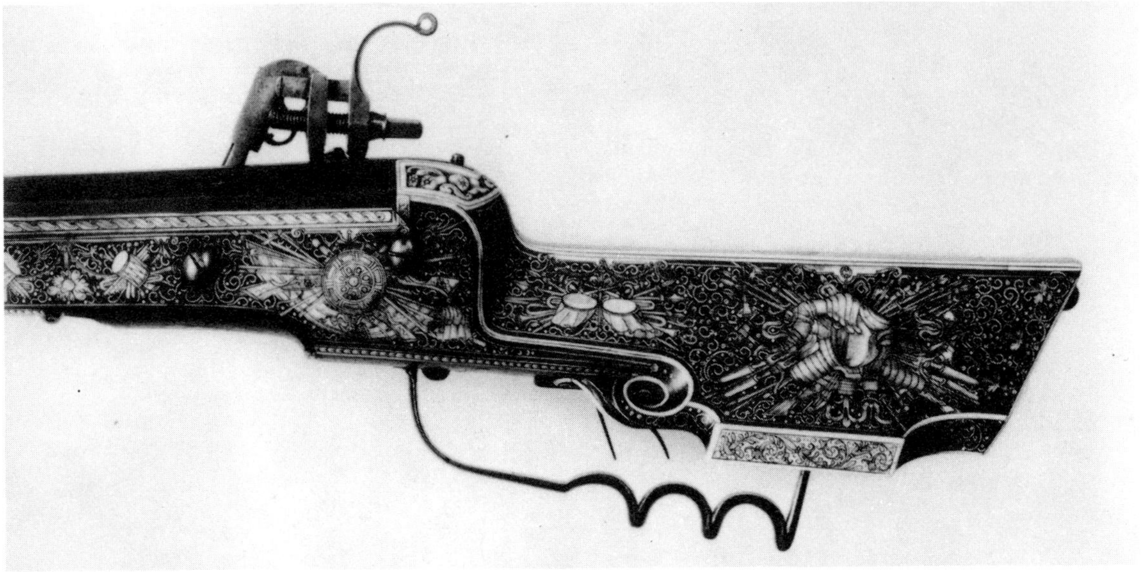

German wheel-lock rifle, dated 1611–12. The walnut stock, decorated in German style, is inlaid with decoration of engraved stag's horn in the form of elephants, deer, etc., with a finely engraved trophy of arms on the butt. *Courtesy Wallace Collection, London, England.*

strate their suitability for their owners, because in most cases the owner or user is unknown. However, we can point to just one or two guns and say that they would have fitted the persons who carried them. A wheel-lock pistol, presented by Frederick II of Denmark to his cousin, August I, Elector of Saxony, a warrior for religion's sake, is decorated with horn plaques carved with the royal arms of Denmark, scenes of warfare, and religious imagery, including pictures of the Risen Christ and Adam and Eve.

Apart from the few categories we have mentioned, the range of ornament employed by gun stockers was almost unlimited. It included pictures of folk in contemporary Polish or Turkish costume, abstractions such as Truth, or Justice, the classical deities such as Mars or Justice, jousters, biblical figures such as Judith, historical personages such as Lucretia, and many more motifs. Often the most diverse ideas in ornamentation would be found together in the ornamentation of just one piece. Thus one stock of a wheel-lock gun of about 1615, made in Saxony, was inlaid with scrolls and flowers, grotesques, a lion rampant, a double eagle, Jupiter, Venus and Cupid, a picture of a lady in contemporary court dress, Orpheus, and Flora and a female caryatid.

Seldom has so much decoration been concentrated on such a small space as on the gun stocks of the sixteenth and seventeenth century. Nor is it difficult to see why this should be the case. If you were able to afford a gun you would easily be able to afford to have it decorated by the finest craftsmen. Overall decoration not only protected the wood, as has already been noted, it provided a better grip for the shooter, because the horn inlay protruded ever so slightly from the wooden surface.

How did the gun stocker achieve his masterly effects? Although no contemporary text has described how he set to work, it is possible to reconstruct the methods he used. He began with some kind of master design. Often this might be provided by the gun barrel itself, as sometimes inlay designs reproduced those damascened or carved on the steel. The stocker might also have before him a pattern book, often of engraved designs which had been published so that they could be utilized

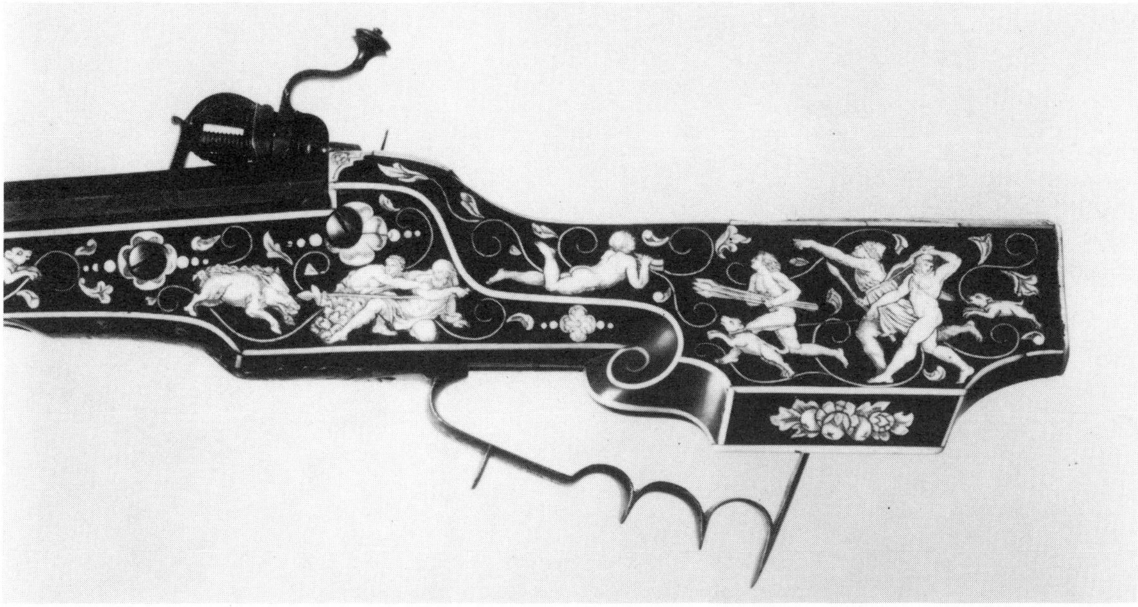

Wheel-lock rifle stock made by "V.D." about 1680. The stock is of snake-wood inlaid with stag's horn, showing hunting scenes with classical figures, with foliated scrolls and tendrils and a running design of deer and boar pursued by hounds. *Courtesy Wallace Collection, London, England.*

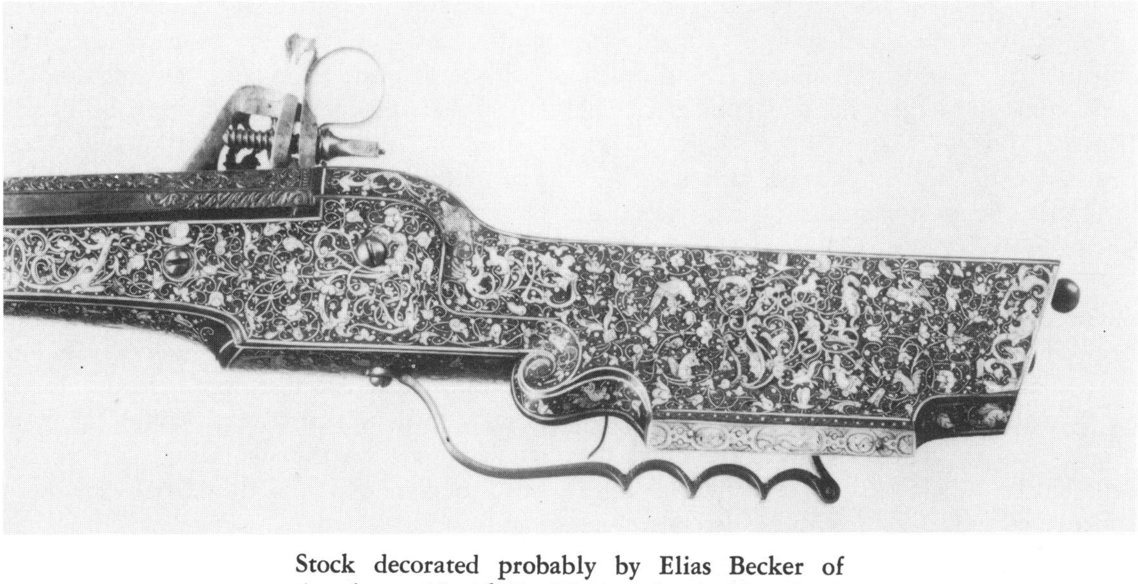

Stock decorated probably by Elias Becker of Augsburg (d. 1679). The stock of this wheel-lock rifle of 1650, which was probably made in Saxony, and which appears in another plate is inlaid with interlacing floral scrolls interspersed with birds, squirrels and grotesque terminal figures. *Courtesy Wallace Collection, London, England.*

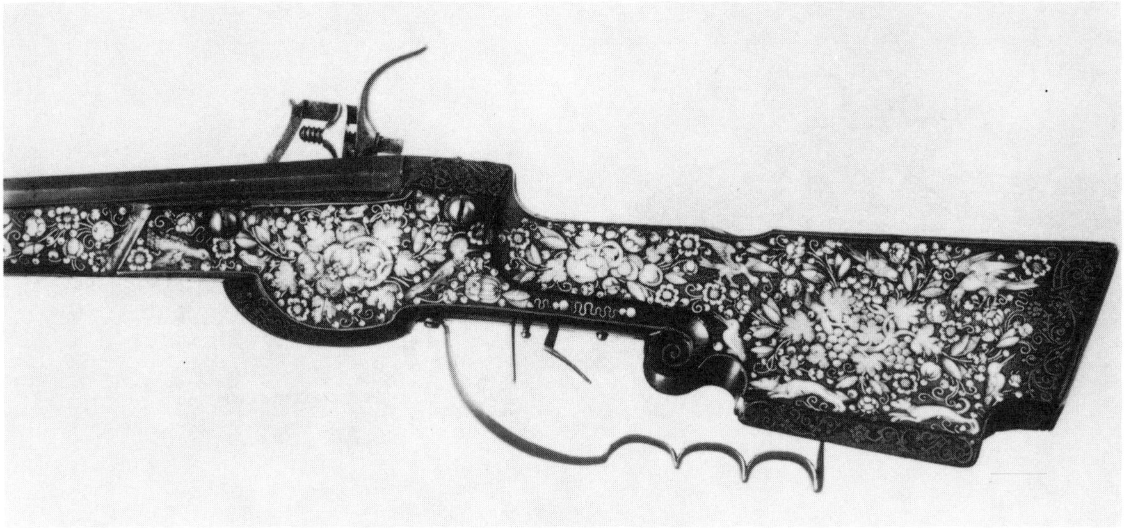

Wheel-lock rifle stock, which was made by J. C. Tornier of Massevaux (Alsace) and which is dated 1645. Here the butt is shown. It is made of Italian walnut decorated in the German fashion and inlaid in engraved stag's horn with scenes of the chase among flowers and foliage. *Courtesy Wallace Collection, London, England.*

in the applied arts. The stock itself would probably have been shaped and smoothed for him by an apprentice, and it is worth noting that the stocks, both of pistols and rifles, seem to have been designed to accommodate themselves to as much inlay as possible by exhibiting the largest possible number of flat surfaces, on which it would be easier to insert inlay than on a rounded surface.

The stock itself was usually made from an exotic wood, ebony, walnut, snake wood or palisander wood. If a plain wooden stock were used, then the stock maker would employ the technique, not of inlay, but marquetry, which will be discussed in its place.

With the size and the shape of the surfaces he was to inlay very much in mind the gun stocker would design the individual inlay pieces with which it was to be decorated and mark out the places for them on the stock. Next he would saw thin plates of stag's horn with a fine toothed saw, seeking those parts of the antlers where there was the greatest amount of spread, such as the juncture of the tines. The stagshorn used might well be a trophy supplied by the patron from some previous hunting expedition. As well as antlers, the stocker would use dyed horn, bone, mother of pearl, ivory, silver and brass wire.

The shapes of the inlay pieces which the stocker now cut from the plate of horn with a thin saw blade in a bow saw, consisted of large square plaques, roundels, irregular shaped figures, and thin spirals or curlicues of horn. The latter type of decoration had probably been suggested by the task of shaping and smoothing horn plaques. The trimming down of a thin horn plaque with a spokeshave, a plane, or a knife, would produce thin shavings of horn which would, of themselves, roll into a spiral shape. All that was necessary to do to inlay them was to draw a similar but more regular spiral on the gun stock, cut out the wood underneath it, and press in the horn spiral.

Having got all the inlay pieces ready, the stocker now laid them on the places marked on the wood, and drew round them with a sharp scriber, to make sure they were a precise fit. Next he cut around the shapes of the inlay piece with the point of a sharp knife, and made a second cut up to the line so that

Sixteenth-century German powder horn, made from a stag's antler and carved with the figures of Adam and Eve. *Courtesy Victoria and Albert Museum, London, England.*

Wooden coffer inlaid with horn. Signed by Jean Conrad Tornier of Massevaux, Alsace, and dated 1630. ***Courtesy Wallace Collection, London, England.***

he was left with a V-shaped cut which completely outlined the shape of the inlay piece. He would then cut down with gouges into the wood so that there was a hollow excavated the exact size of the inlay and the depth of its thickness. Before the inlay piece was laid in place, the stocker would engrave it with a graver and rub some pigment, such as powdered coal mixed with oil, into the lines to make them stand out. A contemporary print of a crossbow maker at work shows on his bench a selection of chisels and gravers of various sorts. He is sharpening a graver on an oil stone as he works at the crossbow, while two large knives also lie on the bench. To cut the recesses for long, very thin, lines of horn inlay, a stocker would use a saw, probably the contemporary kind of hand saw which looks like a large bread knife, and force them well in. Horn inlay set in this fashion can be seen on the butt of one of the guns of the Wallace Collection which has suffered damage.

All that now remained to do was to sink the inlay plaques into their recesses. A little hot glue was spread on the bottom of the recess, which had been left rough, and the inlay plate was laid on it and tapped into place with a non-metallic hammer, which would not splinter or deface the horn.

Only very occasionally did the gun stocker adopt a completely different technique from what has been described and use marquetry instead of inlay. Instead of the inlay pieces being laid directly into recesses cut in the solid body of the stock, the wooden carcass of the stock, formed of some ordinary kind of wood such as deal, was covered with a mo-

This German gaming board, which dates from the second half of the sixteenth century, is veneered with engraved stag's horn and ebony. It is very much in the style of contemporary gunstock decorations, and was almost certainly made by a gunstocker. *Courtesy Victoria and Albert Museum, London, England.*

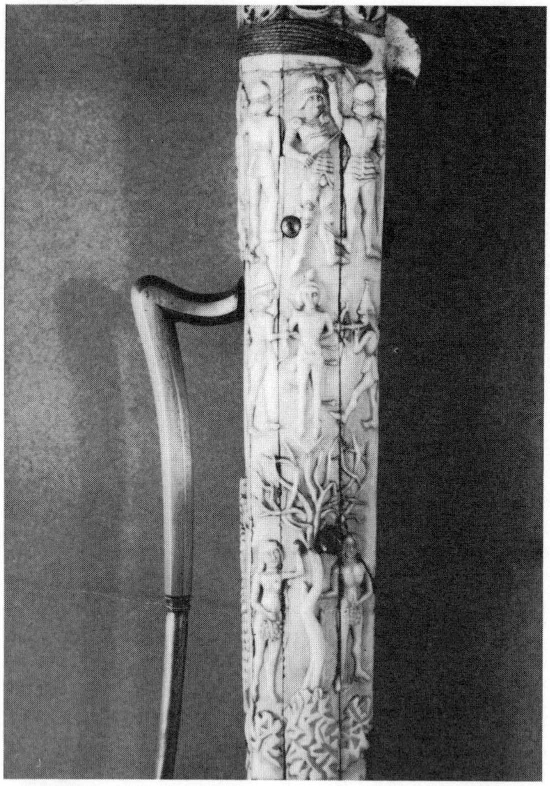

Detail of Fels-Colonna crossbow, showing three armed men in full Gothic armor, the martyrdom of St. Sebastian, and Adam and Eve. Themes taken from war and religion were to be just as popular with gun stockers as they had been with crossbow decorators. *Courtesy Wallace Collection, London, England.*

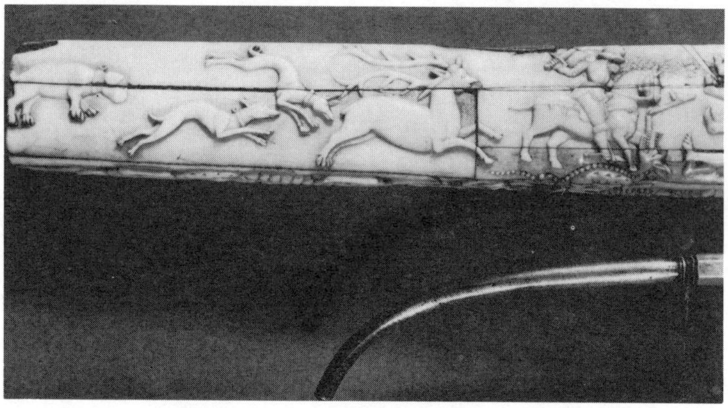

Detail of Fels-Colonna crossbow. Hounds pursue a stag, and St. George slays the Dragon. Hunting and patron saints were themes which would find favor with the gunstock makers. *Courtesy Wallace Collection, London, England.*

Detail of Fels-Colonna crossbow. A maiden is enticed by Folly from Wisdom, youths and maidens dance, or disport themselves in the nude. Erotic themes such as this were to reappear on the firearms for which crossbow makers laid down the decorative tradition. *Courtesy Wallace Collection, London, England.*

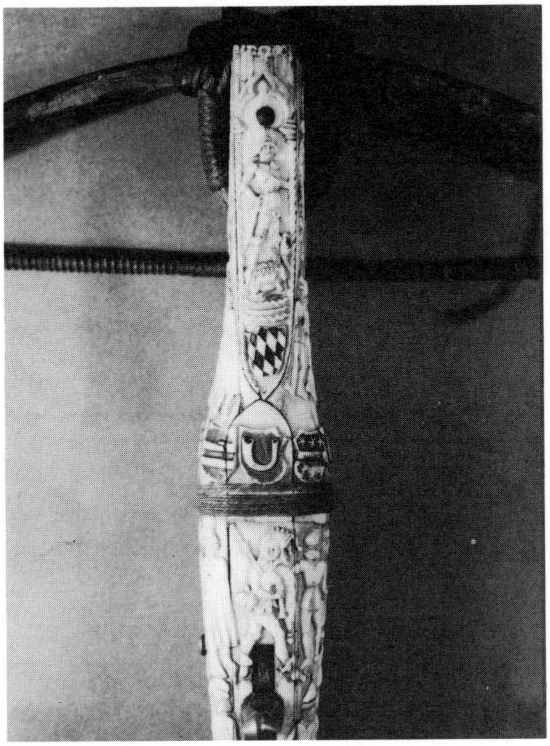

Crossbow inlaid with polished stag's horn, carved in relief in the manner of Master E.S. (an engraver who flourished around 1460) and his follower Israhel van Meckenem. Once the property of the Fels-Colonna family. *Courtesy Wallace Collection, London, England.*

Crossbow, German, about 1650. The fine scrolls of stag's horn with which the stock is decorated could have started life as shavings from the gun stocker's plane. Deer and hounds run riot on this fine piece, which shows how similar the decorations of crossbows and guns were. *Courtesy Wallace Collection, London, England.*

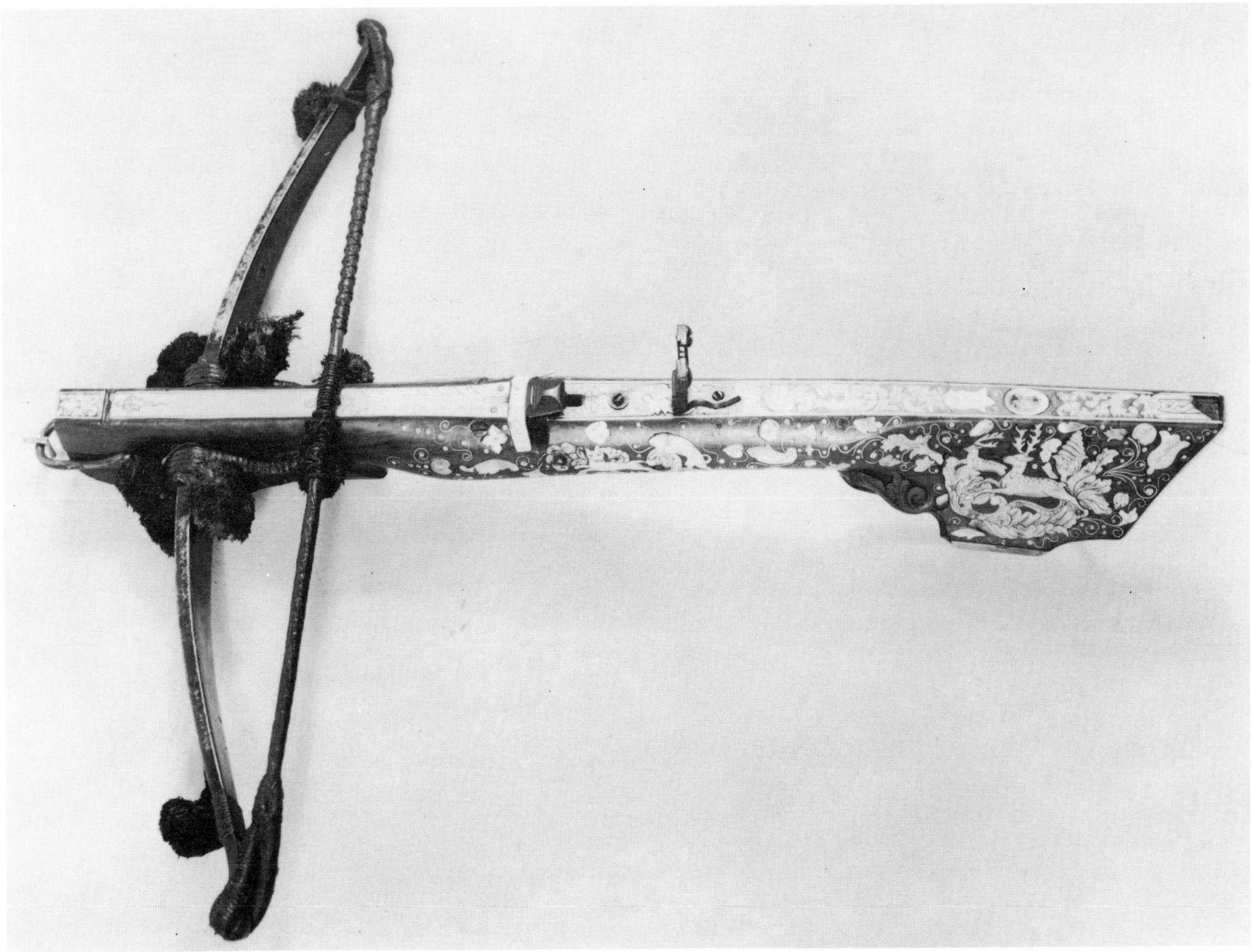

saic of thin pieces of exotic wood, bone, and horn veneer. The sheets of veneer would be laid on top of one another and the pattern sawed through the resulting sandwich with a fine piercing saw. Each design element would thus fit exactly into the space left for it on the sheet below. The whole composition, softened by steeping it in hot water or even boiling, would then be glued onto the wooden gunstock and bound firmly in place until it dried.

Particular attention was paid to certain parts of the stock. The cheek piece showed up once a gun was laid on a rack; it was consequently covered with lavish ornament, which usually included the coat of arms or monogram of the owner. The sliding cover of the butt trap, a compartment which held essential tools for overhauling the gun, had to be made of solid horn, for if it were of wood, the wood might warp because it would have to be made from a thin section. It was usually elaborately carved. Solidity was also essential in the case of the butt, which again was often of solid horn. Most owners were justifiably pessimistic about the reliability of their ignition systems, and guns had to be so designed that if they were inefficient firing weapons, they might at least serve as efficient clubs.

9
THE BONE OF CONTENTION
Prisoner Carving

BONE carving in Europe, during modern times, is dominated by the work done by prisoners of war in England during the Revolutionary and Napoleonic Wars. The men who carved the wonderful toys and models that characterize this epoch were essentially folk artists. In many ways bone is essentially a folk art material; it is inexpensive and the tools required to fashion it are not costly. The artists of the prison camps would not have achieved the results which they did if they had not had some instruction in art, however. This instruction came from a few professional workers in bone whom a variety of forces swept into the great conflicts which raged in America and Europe from the middle of the eighteenth down to the beginning of the nineteenth centuries.

What professional carvers existed during this period? The most numerous of all bone and horn workers were comb makers. Until about the third quarter of the eighteenth century, most English comb makers had been resident in Yorkshire or the Midlands. Then increased demand caused the establishment of comb makers over most of the country. Comb making was all done by hand, with a special saw, called a *stadda,* or double saw, which used the line separating two teeth as a guide for cutting apart the next two. The best combs had always come from France, however, where hair dressing and comb making had blossomed out into an art at the court of Louis XIV. These combs were made in horn and carved in open work. French prisoners (who presumably included some comb workers) were going to make combs exactly like them in the prisons.

There were lots of other French craft workers in horn and bone. Louis Moreri, writing in 1697 about the uses of baleen and whalebone, commented: "out of whalebone, and out of the penis bone of the whale, there are made parasols, fans, staffs for door keepers and gentlemen ushers, corsets and busks for ladies, and various things which turners and cutlers make."[1]

Not all the articles made from bone or whalebone were purely utilitarian. Beautiful snuff rasps were made in France at the beginning of the eighteenth century. These consisted of two carved leaves, with, sandwiched between them, a metal grater. The snuff ad-

1. Louis Moreri, *Le Grand Dictionnaire Historique* Vol. 1 (Paris: Jean Baptiste Coignard, 1725).

Snuffbox of horn made by John Obrisset, a refugee Huguenot craftsman in London. It bears a portrait of Charles I. Obrisset molded the portraits on his snuffboxes by boiling the horn to soften it and applying a metal die. *Courtesy London Museum, Kensington Palace, London, England.*

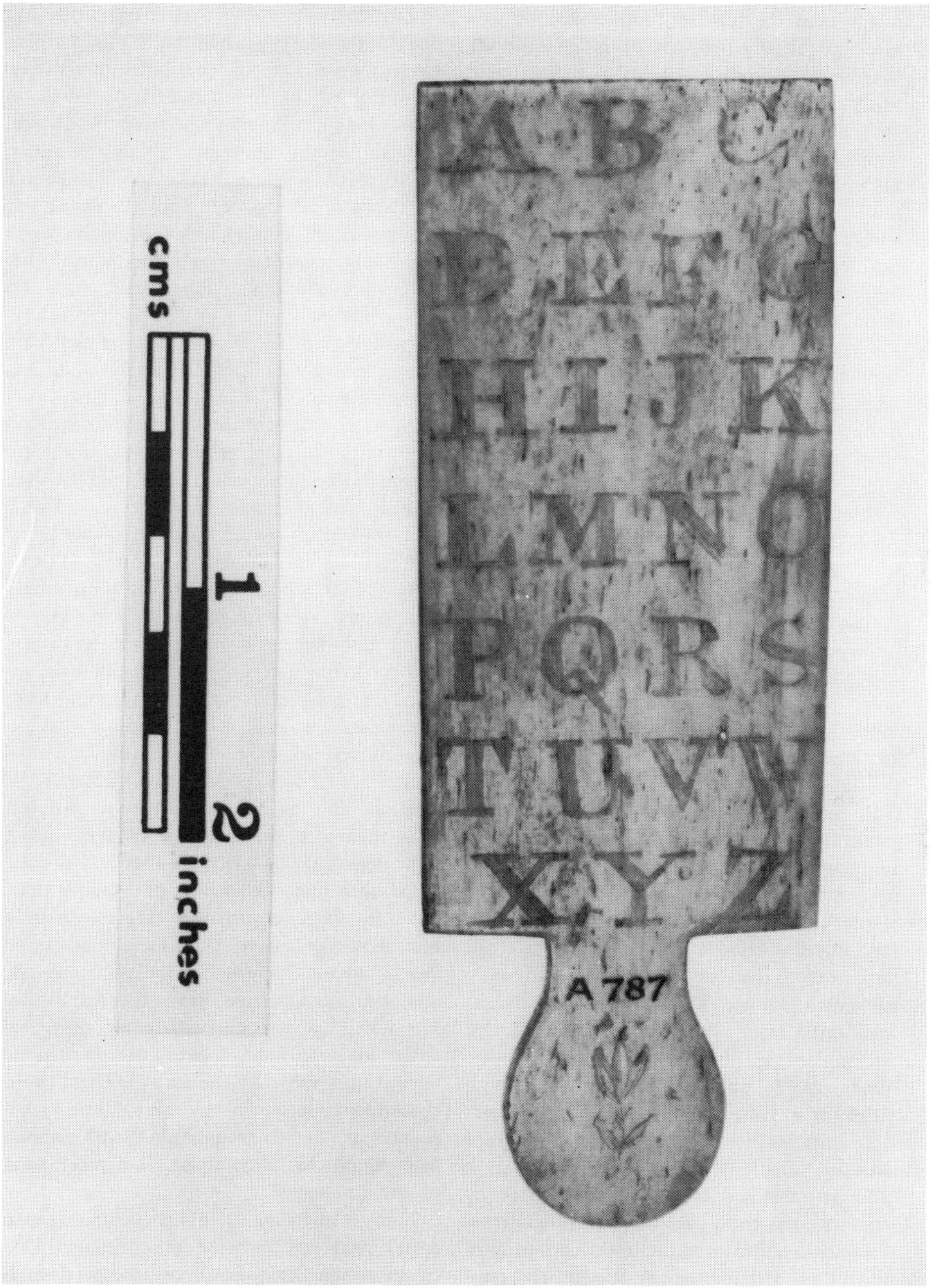

Eighteenth-century hornbook. A hornbook was a transparent piece of horn stuck down on a piece of wood shaped to fit it. Between the horn and the wood was sandwiched a printed alphabet, or, as in this case, the alphabet was engraved directly onto the horn. *Courtesy London Museum, Kensington Palace, London, England.*

dict opened the top leaf, and rubbed on it a made-up roll of cured tobacco, called a *carotte* because of its resemblance to a carrot. Fresh, finely grated snuff fell into a receptacle underneath the grater.

Whalebone workers and horn workers alike made fans, which were usually *brisé,* that is, made of horn or bone sticks joined together with ribbons of silk. The bone sticks of the fan were pierced and fretted by means of drills and piercing saws, and the designs often enhanced by gilding, till they resembled the *mosaique* produced at Dieppe. Coats of arms might appear on the lower parts of the sticks. Minuet fans were also made from perforated horn or bone sticks, but with a large part of the stick left uncut, so as to show several large medallions, which were adorned with paintings.

Other items made from horn included the snuffbox. This included boxes made by pressing horn into a mold, such as those made by the famous French craftsman John Obrisset, who settled in London for religious reasons, and snuffboxes or tobacco boxes inlaid with carved horn plaques. I recently discovered one of these in the London Museum, Kensington Palace, London, England, which is exactly like the very early scrimshaw boxes with walrus ivory plaques which I found in Hull. This snuffbox bears a comparable date, 1708, and and identical motto: "If you love mee lend me nott." In view of this discovery it seems reasonable to assume that the first English scrimshoner began to copy boxes inlaid in horn during the late seventeenth and early eighteenth century. Many other knick-knacks were made from whalebone, including ladies' walking sticks, formed like shepherdesses' crooks, mens' walking sticks, covered with plaited whalebone or rather baleen, and punch ladle handles, formed of a twisted strip of baleen.

Besides the busks, such as those made by later scrimshoners, which went into foundation garments, regular couturier-made corsets were stiffened with thin plates of baleen. The fashion in corsets varied over the years. Sometimes they were worn outside the dress, sometimes within. During an era when outside wear was fashionable a Scottish beadle used to take his seat on a flat table-top tomb, just outside the door of his church, as morning service began. One by one, ladies in the congregation whom tight-lacing had caused to faint would be brought out from the church, and laid on the tombstone. With one sweep of his clasp-knife the beadle would then cut all the laces on the outside of the corset and thus restore the fashion-conscious worshipper to life. Many prisoner of war models contain baleen, work which may have been contributed by staymakers who got caught up in the Revolutionary and Napoleonic wars, as did Tom Paine, author of *The Rights Of Man* and *Common Sense.*

All sorts of obscure workers passed on their skills to the prison artists, including French cutlers who made bone knife handles. French button makers had been at work since the twelfth century. They made five-holed bone buttons on a lathe, piercing them with a hand drill which left the holes irregularly spaced, and smoothing them down with a rough file. Hair plait workers, who wove hair into cords for watch chains (usually hair donated by sweethearts and wives) must have contributed the skill which made it possible for prisoners to twist human hairs into miniature cables for model ships. Thomas R. Beaufort, an English antiquary who re-rigged very many of the prisoner of war model ships during the nineteen-twenties and thirties, found that just one shroud of a ship's mast contained thirty human hairs. These hairs only became visible under a magnifying glass; to the naked eye the shrouds looked as though they had been woven from the finest silk. The texture was so close that they were perfectly to scale, and looked exactly like a thick ship's cable in miniature. There were about sixty such shrouds on a ship model and it would have taken 1800 human hairs to provide them, apart from other parts of the rigging.

Many American scrimshoners must have found their way into the prison camps. One of the regular scrimshaw motifs is the clasped-hand walking stick handle. This is also found among the Dieppe ivory carvers, who, as will be seen in a moment, had strong connections with the prison camps. It may have reached

An English painting showing the bargaining which took place in prisoner of war camps for the prisoners' handicrafts. Bone trinkets as well as straw plait are being sold. Note the French prisoner on the right holding up two fingers to show the price of the model he is holding, because he does not speak English and the purchaser does not speak French. *Courtesy Luton Art Gallery.*

Dieppe from New Bedford, via Forton, where many Americans were interned. "Going to make bone ships at Forton," became American mercantile marine slang for being captured by a British cruiser.

Even the British may have contributed towards prisoner of war work, because the idea of carving the meat bones left over from your meal is apparently originally a British idea, not a French one. There is a record of one dinner guest, after the meal, calling for the left over bones. When they were brought he produced a pocket lathe and turned them into toys and gimcracks which he gave away to the children of the house and his fellow guests. Frenchmen were hardly likely to have tried carving leftover bones before they came to England, as the average Frenchman never got any meat. Professional ivory and bone carvers such as the Dieppois, however, had long been familiar with bone as a carving material. A visitor to the port in 1775 had remarked that ivory carving in France was much less prosperous than it had been. Patrons had begun to dislike ivory, because it turned yellow, and because marquetry (another speciality of Dieppe, which appears on the baseboard stands of prisoner of war model ships, and Dieppe ivory ships) was a powerful counter attraction. Nonetheless, he went on, many ivory carvers in Dieppe continued in work, making many small objects such as snuffboxes and open wotk needle cases. Some of the carvers had woken up to the virtues of bone, "the use of which ought to be encouraged because we produce it ourselves." There was more carving to be got out of a beefbone than any other kind of bone, and

Prisoner of war bone model ship, made by American or French prisoners of war in England. The ship is the H.M.S. *Mars,* 74 guns, launched 1794.
Courtesy The Parker Gallery, London, England.

it grew less yellow than ivory, though it was more fragile. Horse bone was the hardest, it was of a dazzling whiteness. Sheep's bones were also in use, he adds. As Normandy had been an essentially sheep raising country, into which oxen had made a very belated entry, carving from sheep's bones had probably preceded work in all other kinds of bone. There can be little doubt that it was the prisoners from Dieppe who provided the skilled instruction necessary to train the other prisoners to produce bone work. Hitherto the connection between Dieppe and the British prison camps has been largely a speculative one, based on similarities of style between Dieppois and prison work. I have now fortunately been able to establish a direct connection. In the Chateau Museum at Dieppe there is a watch stand, a sort of miniature clock case, in which men used to hang their pocket watch when they went to bed, so that it could be seen, at a glance, during the night. This watch stand is carved with the supporters to the British Royal Arms, the Lion and the

Prisoner of war bone model ship. Note the riveting. ***Courtesy Christies, London, England.***

Unicorn. Obviously a design of this sort was intended to appeal principally to British patrons, and it must have been one which a Dieppe carver brought back with him from a prison camp.

The best description of prison artists at work has been given by an American prisoner, George Little. "The French," he writes, "brought themselves systematically to some pursuit; they manufactured a variety of articles, such as a straw plait for bonnets, bone work of various descriptions, instruments of music, and miniature ships, which were bought up by the country people or exchanged for their produce." Considerable rewards awaited the successful bone worker. "These French prisoners," Little writes, "had become so thoroughly reconciled to their situation (some of them having been here six and eight years) that their minds appeared to be wholly occupied with gain. I knew many of them, who, when peace was effected between France and England, had saved from one to two thousand guineas and there were some who did not actually wish to leave the prison." Many other accounts confirm that the best bone carvers were high-

Prisoner of war bone model ship, H.M.S. *Indefatigable,* 64 guns. Note baleen strakes. *Courtesy Christies, London, England.*

ly paid. At Greenlaw "some were manufacturing the cast-away bones into dice, dominoes, paper cutters, and a hundred articles of toy-work, and realised considerable sums of money." The prisoners' world was so topsy-turvy that the artists had more money than anyone else. How different from the world outside! If you wanted to change money, or raise a loan, you approached a bone carver. "I exchanged part of my French gold for English money," wrote an anonymous Frenchman who was planning an escape from Norman's Cross, "with those of my comrades who, by making toys and fancy work, which they were allowed to dispose of for their own benefit, had got a little together."[2]

An artist had many difficulties to overcome before he could even start work, however. Like Charles Herbert of Newburyport in Massachusetts, for example, who had been captured aboard the *Dolton* in 1776, when the prison-

2. Chambers, *Miscellany*.

Prisoner of war bone model ship. The detail of the 74-gun ship is characteristic of prisoner work. The figurehead, anchors, capstan, bollards, companion way, handrails, hatch covers, catheads, ship's boats and carved poop were all carved separately. *Courtesy Christies, London, England.*

English seventeenth-century folk art bone carving, a shoehorn inscribed: "Thomas Gen: Made This for L.W." ***Courtesy British Museum, London, England.***

er of war era started, he might be still recovering from wounds or illness. Herbert recovered, was sent to Mill Prison, and went to the Sunday market every week to sell his boxes, spoons and punch ladles. The carver also had to begin by teaming up with one of his fellow prisoners, as most prison work was done on a cooperative basis. Success as an artist depended not merely on talent, but also on an ability to get on with other people. He had to buy his tools: a drill, a pair of pliers, a small saw, glue, silk for the rigging of models, brass wire for pinning planking to a hull, and a thicker wire for the guns. He also needed to buy his raw material bones, because he could not hope to accumulate enough from the meals he ate himself, even though the British government contractor did his best to oblige him by supplying as many bones with the meat as he possibly could so as to increase his profit. The bones were bought either from the cookhouse or from fellow prisoners. Doisy, a French prisoner who made ornaments, knick-knacks, boxes, combs, toys, and especially ship models at Forton from the bones in his food, recalls that beef and mutton bones were carefully saved on all sides, and that those who could not work them sold them at good prices to those who could. If the prison at which the artist was held captive had a market where country folk came regularly to sell their produce and buy prisoners' wares, all he had to do was to set up his stall there. This usually meant taking a seat with his products on a tray on his knees and waiting for buyers. Some prisons did not have markets and artists imprisoned in those particular gaols found life much more difficult. At Edinburgh Castle, for example there was only a narrow space

French snuff graters, made in the eighteenth century. To the right Venus and Cupid, to the left the Judgment of Solomon. ***Courtesy Victoria and Albert Museum, London, England.***

between the palisades through which the prisoners could hand out their bone work and receive payment in exchange. Sometimes the prisoners' visits to the market resulted in romantic encounters. At the Golden Tower prison at Pembroke in Wales, two girls fell in love with two handsome Frenchmen whom they had seen among the prisoners, selling their manufactures at the daily market. They contrived to smuggle into the prison some shin bones of horses and cows, which the prisoners shaped into digging tools. They tunneled

Eighteenth-century French snuff graters. To the left a lady in oriental costume, to the right a lawyer. His sleeve hears the legend: "Apointe Mentor Dinaire." *Courtesy Victoria and Albert Museum, London, England.*

Seventeenth-century horn tumbler. Note the borders, which prefigure later scrimshaw decoration. ***Courtesy Victoria and Albert Museum, London, England.***

their way out of the prison, and escaped with the girls on Lord Cawdor's yacht, which was moored close by, and succeeded in slipping into St. Malo. If there was no market, a prisoner would have to bribe his guards to smuggle out his bone carvings. The only occasion when the authorities interfered with this smuggling was when the prisoners were constructing obscene toys to satisfy "the depraved taste of some of the British purchasers." Miniature models of scenes of an erotic nature, sometimes concealed in an egg which was hinged and opened, had long been made in France. In 1798 the Prison Authorities at London ordered that: "Obscene figures and indecent toys, and all such indecent representations tending to disseminate Lewdness and Immorality exposed for sale, or prepared for that purpose, are to be instantly destroyed."[3] This proclamation had little effect and in 1808 the prison market at Norman's Cross was closed down. The prisoners' letters were

3. Jane Toller, *Prisoner of War Work, 1756–1815* (Cambridge: Golden Head Press, 1965).

opened and a Corporal Haynes of the guard and a prisoner called "Black Jimmy" were discovered to be the ringleaders in the smuggling of obscene toys. They were punished and the market reopened. There was only one other occasion, apart from those which I have mentioned, on which the prison authorities interfered with the bone carvers. This was when some prisoners in Scotland were found to have carved a bone block from which bank notes could be printed.

Prison toys, models, and knick-knacks are very varied in their range. They all, however, bear a distinct stamp of prison handiwork, even when the prison artist has deliberately set out to copy a model from outside the prison, such as Russian ivory boxes, which were widely imitated. Identification of a piece as prison handiwork is determined partly by the nature of the material, and the object made, which was sometimes exclusive to the prison artist, such as the ship model, only a few examples of which, none of them in bone, are known to have been made outside prisons. The prisoners' handiwork is finished off in rough material. A work box, for example, made in imitation of a Russian ivory box with a pierced·top, may be lined with rather cheap, coarse colored paper. Sometimes a model is trimmed with straw plait of the very fine variety, which was again a prison speciality. Usually there is the indefinable air of folk art work about any piece of prison handicraft.

Prisoners' pieces include mechanical toys, worked by a series of ratchets and pulleys when a handle is turned. On one toy group turning a wheel below the platform on which the figures stand sets a lady winding wool, a child moving, a soldier and another lady waltzing, a mother tossing her baby up in the air, while she looks at yet another lady who is preparing tea. Other models and toys include a law court and a theater, the walls and scenery formed of very finely pierced and fretted bone, looking like Dieppe *mosaique* or Chinese tracery on a wedding junk. We must not forget that Chinese models were copied in the prisons, and one American artist sold many "Chinese" wood carvings in Plymouth and Moretonhampstead. Guillotine

Early nineteenth-century American scrimshawed button.

models, complete with the condemned man strapped to a plank, spare human heads in a basket, executioners and soldiers, and painted gore on the knife of the guillotine, were very popular. Cribbage boards and domino boxes were in great demand from patrons. Some of the prison artists may have been domino makers in civilian life, like the Dieppois, who were famous for making miniature dominoes which would pack into a model sabot. Watch stands (such as the one in the Chateau Museum at Dieppe) chessmen, fans, tobacco stoppers, apple scoops, seals, knitting needles, lace bobbins, thimbles, and tobacco boxes were all parts of the repertoire of the prison artist.

The most prized pieces, then and now, are the model ships. It took two prisoners at Forton over six months to complete a large-sized model, and the work of building it was broken down between the two of them. Looking at an average prisoner model it is possible to analyze the different tasks that had to be carried out. First of all the hull had to be shaped, and the thin planks of bone, previously sawn from a beef bone, pinned to it by means of short lengths of brass wire. Then the whole surface had to be made smooth and unified. Sometimes the modeller was able to save himself work by using very long lengths of bone for the strakes. These might be as long as eighteen inches, and they were obviously cut from horse or cow shin bones. The modeller would also introduce strips of baleen, which is easier to bend and work than bone. Whenever possible, a modeller carved a fitting as a whole, rather than building it up from small pieces. He would carve the whole of the sides of the stern gallery out of one piece of bone, and do the same with the balustrades, the ladders, the boats, the ship's bell and its canopy, and any other part of the ship which lent itself to this treatment.

With all the labor-saving devices available, the amount of work required to make a prisoner of war model was still enormous. On a middling sized model 3021 pins would be required just to pin the bone planks to the hull. As the model was intended to catch a likely patron's eye, it had, above all, to be ornamental. The stern windows had to be filled in with gold paper, the gunports painted red inside (a custom the British Navy had adopted so that blood stains would not be too conspicuous during battle) and a marquetry stand had to be made, ornamented with bone balustrades and carved animals.

One of the marvels of the prisoner of war model was that the carvers were able to make it without plans, and perhaps without any knowledge of the sea, or ships. Most of the French prisoners were soldiers, landsmen whose only experience at sea had been a trip, battened down under hatches, from wherever they had been captured, to England. They were, however, able to make models of other objects which they had never seen, such as Spinning Jennies, a special kind of machine used in English textile factories. There were only two or three of these in France and it is very unlikely that any prisoner was allowed to see any of those working in English factories.

Beaufort believed that many of the model ships were special commissions, ordered by the relatives of officers serving in the navy, who wanted a model of their kinsman's ship. The most romantic commission for a model ship, which is now owned by a friend of M. René Bazin, the Curator of the Chateau Museum at Dieppe, was placed by some English ladies. They had been captured at sea by the famous French privateer Surcouf. French Privateers at that time had a bad reputation; the fair captives expected a fate worse than death, then death itself. However, Surcouf treated them with the utmost chivalry, and returned them, unharmed, to British hands. As a reward for what the privateer had done, or as M. Bazin puts it, "for what he had not done," the ladies commissioned a bone ship as a present for the French captain, and had it rigged with strands of their hair so that their gallant captor would always have something to remind him of his former prisoners.

10

HORNS OF ABUNDANCE

Far Eastern Carving

THE story of every art must begin somewhere; there can be little doubt that the story of Chinese horn carving begins in milady's chamber. All Chinese of rank or wealth were accustomed, nay, expected to maintain several wives, and several concubines as well. In an endeavor to avoid losing "face" before his women folk, the much-married Chinese had become more and more preoccupied with the search for stronger and stronger aphrodisiacs. Eventually this search ended with the discovery of Borneo, an island which, according to Chinese ideas, was the Eldorado of virility renewers.

"There is to be found there," writes Bruzen de la Martiniere in 1768, "a great quantity of those birds' nests which the Chinese, and several other nationalities, value so highly that they will pay three hundred pieces of eight for one *Pico,* as they are called, imagining that it will produce a strong stimulation to the begetting of children and help a great deal towards it . . . the sensual Chinese buy, for the same purpose, shark's fins, which fish are found in the waters around this island and they will pay for them forty pieces of eight a *pico.* This means that the Mandarins swallow a great deal of gold in a few bites, because they only eat the small sinews, as they do those of the deer . . . The wild men, or *Beajous* procure from monkeys, some red, some black and white, called *Oncas* the best Bezoar stones in the world. They shoot the monkeys with their darts lightly, so that the animals do not die straight away, but while this wound makes them feeble and ill, the stone forms in their entrails, and they kill them to obtain it." For some reason de la Martiniere does not mention *the* aphrodisiac which the Chinese obtained from Borneo, rhinoceros horn, but he does make an oblique reference to the other magical substance which was sought after by the Chinese—hornbill. 'They try to obtain certain pointed horns, which they polish, and then carry as an ornament for their belt."

Two of these animal treasures the Chinese believed, in addition to their power of conferring sexual potency, could repel the effects of poison, bezoar stones and rhinoceros horn. Both these qualities would make them extremely interesting to a rich Mandarin, whose jealous wife, or concubine, often administered to him what was euphemistically called in China, "the white powder death."

The wonderful stories told to the Chinese

by the Malay traders on the coast, who in turn had heard them from the "wild men," simple folk who were nonetheless adept at getting the maximum price for their wares and keeping their sources of supply secret, had induced in them a firm belief in the occult virtues of rhinoceros and hornbill horn.

Both the horn of the rhinoceros, and the projection of the hornbill were not really necessary to the creatures' physical makeup, rather they were characteristics of male sexuality, like the horn of the narwhal, which also serves no useful purpose and which was also supposed to be an infallible detector of poisons.

The task of exploiting this animal wealth was left to the wild men of the interior, people whom modern anthropologists would now differentiate into many different tribes: Punans, Ibans, Kanyans, Dayaks, and others. To the Malay traders of the coast, Mohammedan immigrants who kept the interior folk in subjection, with their steel weapons and firearms, they all seemed much of a muchness, hopeless pagan savages.

Bruzen de la Martiniere paints another, rather more glowing picture of the inhabitants of upland Borneo. "This people," he says "do not worship any idols and the sacrifices which they make of aromatic woods and incense are offered to God alone, who, they believe, will recompense the good with His glory and punish the wicked in Hell. They marry but one wife and regard lack of faith in marriage, on one side or the other, as so hateful a crime that they punish it with death. The women are modest and retiring, the men enemies of theft and fraud, and grateful for whatever good actions are done to them. They live together in great charity and harmony, there is something noble even in their pleasures, they love to acquire honour in the chase."[1]

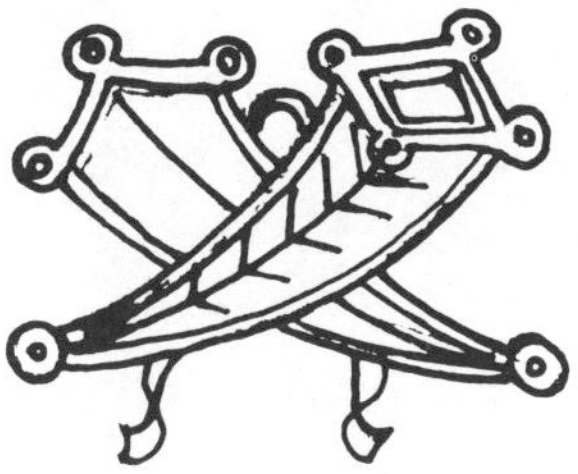

Rhinoceros horn cups, Chinese symbols of happiness.

The principal way of acquiring honor in the chase for a Punan, Iban, Kanyan, or Dayak was to bring back a human head. No properly brought up maiden would dream of yielding her virginity to a youth who had not collected at least one head, and the more heads he had acquired, the more attractive he became. The Punans, a simple folk who for untold centuries had wandered through the jungle, pausing at night to build overnight shelters, cooking their meals of wild *sago,* fruits of the forest and game on campfires, and singing melancholy songs while they wove their rattan mats, held a considerable lead over their neighbors in the matter of headhunting. Their eight-foot-long blowguns, which they ingeniously bored for themselves from a length of hardwood, would bring down anything that moved within a range of twenty paces, transfixing it with a dart poisoned with the juice of the Ipoh tree.

Fear of the Punans helped to keep up the price of rhinoceros horn and hornbill, while tales of the terrors of the jungle helped to add to the mystique which surrounded these two exotics. Originally rhinoceros had been hunted in Yung Ch'ang Gu, and other parts of the province of Yunnan in China, and also on the borders of Annam and Siam, where both the one-horned Indian, and the two-horned Sumatran rhinoceros were found. By quite an early period, however, Chinese cultivation and the firing of forests to drive game had reduced much of the country to a treeless desert quite

1. Bruzen De La Martiniere, *Le Grand Dictionnaire Géographique* Vol. 1 (Paris, 1768), p. 73.

Napoleon's present to Josephine. Chinese bone and ivory model of a rock garden, early nineteenth century. *Courtesy Victoria and Albert Museum, London, England.*

Napoleon's present to Josephine. Early nineteenth-century Chinese model of a palace. *Courtesy Victoria and Albert Museum, London, England.*

incapable of supporting beasts of the chase. New supplies had to be found overseas, and horns from Borneo, Sumatra, Annam, Cambodia, Siam, Champa, Java, Malacca, Kelantan, and Johore found their way to China as trade or tribute.

Both the Indian and the Sumatran rhinoceros were formidable animals. The horn of an Indian rhino, though quite short, could easily impale an elephant or eviscerate a whole line of picketed horses. Folds of skin, like plate armor, hung in huge flaps over the rhino's shoulders, protecting them from a direct spear thrust. The surest, yet the most dangerous

Japanese *netsuke* of bone and wood, depicting a performing monkey. Signed "Miwa," and made in the eighteenth century. *Courtesy Victoria and Albert Museum, London, England.*

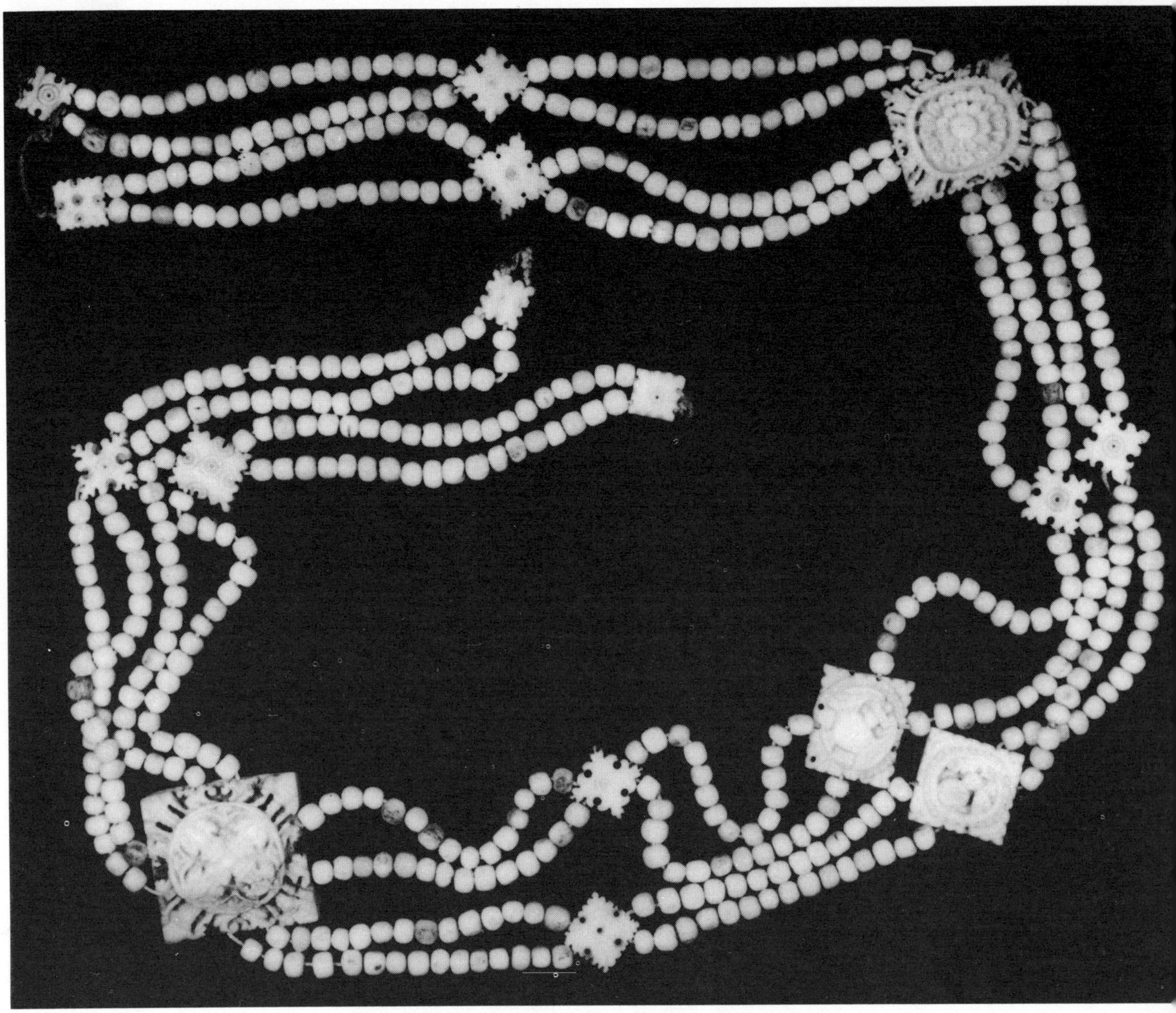

Tibetan rosary of the Black Hat magician sect made from human bone. ***Courtesy Horniman Museum, Forest Hill, London, England.***

way of killing a rhino was to spear it in the belly, where the skin was thinnest. Ordinary bullets bounced off the hide, which was used for making bullet-proof shields, and only those specially hardened with tin or solder could penetrate it. Although the Sumatran rhino, like its relative, the Javanese variety, was supposed to be slightly less formidable than the ferocious Indian rhinoceros, most hunters were inclined to give it a wide berth. The Semangs of Sumatra preferred to tackle it by waiting until it had been wallowing in a mud bath, and the mud had hardened round its legs so that it could not extricate itself in a hurry. They would then rush up to it as it lay in the swamp, build a fire round it, and burn it to death before it could get out.

The horn of the rhinoceros was not really a horn at all, but a collection of hairs cemented together. It was a mere male hirsute appendage, like the beard in humans. It was composed of minute hairy filaments, like the bristles which edge a piece of baleen. It did not grow from the skull but from the skin;

it was polished and smooth at the tip, but rough and split into numerous filaments at the base. If a section is cut through a rhinoceros horn it can be seen to be composed of numerous hairy filaments lying side by side. If examined under a microscope by polarized light, the section will glow with all the colors of the rainbow and look very similar to a section of real hair, which in a sense it is.

Sumatran rhinoceri had long been famous for the antidotic qualities of their two horns. The local folk and the Chinese alike firmly believed that poison poured into a rhinoceros horn cup would cause effervescence. Ctesias, a physician to the royal house of Persia in the fifth century before Christ, describes the great one-horned Indian rhinoceros and the wonderful medicinal properties of the cups made from its horns. As early as the Han dynasty (206 B.C. to 220 A.D.) rhinoceros horn cups were being brought to China from India by Greek and Roman merchant skippers. It was firmly held by writers of the time that not merely would a white efflorescence appear on the outside of a rhinoceros horn cup into which poison had been poured, but the same phenomenon would appear on a spatula of rhinoceros horn stirred into the liquid to test it, while even shavings of the black opaque horns, not used for carvings, were sold as medicine. Nor were the Chinese blind to the decorative qualities of rhinoceros horn, which has a beautiful mottled appearance comparable to, but not the same as, bird's eye maple. A fourteenth century expert on connoisseurship remarked that there were three main types of horn. Those which were thick and long, transparent, and mottled with pleasant designs were much sought after and correspondingly expensive. The kind known as "mountain horn" was also acceptable; it had small dapplings like grains of millet. Horns which exhibited yellow spots, were valuable, but if the black predominated over the yellow, or if the yel-

Early eighteenth-century writing cabinet in bone, made in India. *Courtesy Victoria and Albert Museum, London, England.*

Top of the Holman Hunt Cabinet. *Courtesy Victoria and Albert Museum, London, England.*

Cabinet of wood mounted with bone, made under Dutch influence in South India or Ceylon during the late seventeenth century. Formerly owned by the English artist Holman Hunt. *Courtesy Victoria and Albert Museum, London, England.*

low was too dark, with spots like wild pepper seeds, the horn was less desirable. The best kind of horn was well marked, with a pattern which could be, imaginatively, identified with particular objects. It should be mottled at the top, with marks like clouds, have spots at the bottom that looked like rain drops, be translucent all through, and show the real rhinoceros horn colors, black or yellow.

Horns which showed unpleasing patterns or which were long, light to the hand, or thin, were rejected. The all-black type of horn was also regarded as being unsuitable for anything except making chessmen (which in China were simple flat discs, with the names of the pieces written on them) or shaving up for medicine. Taste in horns changed somewhat over the years. By the nineteenth century a transparent amber or yellow, veined with black, was in vogue, and most artistic carvings were made in these colors, with reddish horn coming next in preference. Occasionally rhinoceros horn was stained, but not if it were being used for cups. This was so that whatever fluid the cup contained could percolate into the absorbent horn, and become imbued with its wonderful aphrodisiacal virtues.

It is not surprising, in view of the high value set on rhinoceros horns, and the rigorous demands of connoisseurs, that as early as the fourteenth century, a brisk trade had grown up in forging carvings supposed to be made from the genuine Indian or Sumatran article. Sometimes this forgery took the form of imposing a thin layer of rhinoceros horn on a slice of ordinary horn. These horn sandwiches would be used to make up the horn plaques which were the official mountings for Tang Dynasty girdles. They could be detected by searching for the seam where they had been welded together, or turning over the plaque to see whether the graining of the horn was the same on one side as on the other.

Whole horns were also adulterated by having more attractive patterns dyed on them. Here again the experienced collector could detect a fraud by looking to see whether the dappled spots, which are compared to millet, or fish roe, were completely circular. A further fraudulent type of rhinoceros horn carving

Exorciser's horn, Tibet.

was that made from mountain yak. The markings on yak's horn were similar to those made from rhinoceros horn but sufficiently different to be detectable. Since yak's horns were a drug on the market and they were thrown away in Tibet, or used to build walls for houses, there was a great profit to be made by falsifying them and making them appear to be rhinoceros. Yet another kind of horn, which was mysteriously said to be that of a giant snake, the Ku-Tu, provided rhinoceros horn carvings of a sort. They were a pale yellow, red, like jasper, and were supposed to have all the prophylactic properties of genuine rhinoceros horn. They were called "Jasper rhinoceros horns," and were extremely expensive. There was one very effective way of persuading a customer that he had bought a genuine rhinoceros horn cup, and this was to let him pour poison into it and watch it effervesce. Just how this was done is described by an old writer, who saw the Venetians making fake unicorn cups—the unicorn, it will be remembered, was supposed to have the same properties as the rhinoceros—by using shavings of unicorn horn. "Some wicked persons do make a mingle-mangle thereof, being as I hear say compounded with lime and soap, or peradventure with earth, or some stone (which things are aft apt to make bubbles arise) and afterwards sell it for the unicorn's horn." In other words, the fakers took shavings of horn, either of the rhinoceros or some other kind of horn, fused them together and made a molded cup, and lined it with a little soap, so that when poison was poured into it, it would effervesce.

The value set on rhinoceros cups by the Chinese can be seen from their employment as libation vessels for the sacrifices made to the ancestral spirits, the only part of their religion which they took at all seriously. The decoration of these cups, which were carved in Canton by specialist rhinoceros horn carvers, who also worked in other horns and tortoiseshell, was extremely complex, involving many symbolic items of decoration. One cup in the Victoria and Albert Museum in London is decorated with branches of pine and polyphorus fungus, symbols of long life, with the figure of a dragon at the top of a waterfall, and with carp swimming at the bottom. This is a symbol of success at the examinations for state offices; the carp which persists in swimming upstream eventually swims up the waterfall and becomes a dragon, just as the student who passes all his examinations becomes a Mandarin. The wooden stand upon which the cup rests, and which has obviously been made to fit it, has been carved with both Taoist symbols and Buddhist hermits and deities, together with plants and trees emblematic of good fortune and happiness, such as the pine, peach, and bamboo.

Both very large cups, carved from the whole horn, and often called "cornucopias," and smaller libation cups measuring just a few inches high were made. Other carvings include statuettes, snuff bottles, and snuff saucers.

At least by the eighteenth century, a design representing crossed rhinoceros horn cups had become a symbol for happiness. Anyone who did possess two rhinoceros cups was also likely to have most of what the practical and worldly Chinese regarded as the essentials of happiness: wealth, without which he could not have paid for the rare material and the skill of the Cantonese carvers, ancestors to whom he could sacrifice, and a harem of many wives and concubines, possessions which had probably prompted his buying the cups in the first place.

The Roman naturalist, Pliny, had heard a lot about the hornbill, but refused to believe in it. Although he found no difficulty in believing that beavers, pursued by hunters, would lie down on the ground and chew off their testicles (which were widely used in medicine) and leave them for their pursuers, confident they would pursue no further, Pliny says himself: "I can no more believe in gryphons or flying horses, than I can in the *Tragopan* (hornbill) which many men say is larger than an eagle, having crooked horns like a ram on either side of the head."

The more Pliny heard about the hornbill, or to be precise the helmet hornbill (*Rhinoplax vigil*) the less he was likely to believe it. Not merely does the cock bird wall up his mate with mud in the hollow of a tree while she hatches her eggs, during which time he feeds her, but both sexes periodically cast the epithelial layer of their gizzard. What is more, though it is no larger than a swan, the hornbill carries on its head the largest excrescence worn by any bird, an enormous casque, four inches high by two inches broad. It is the only member of the hornbill family whose casque, or bony superstructure, is hard enough to carve. All the others carry a lump of light, cellular bone. The casque borne by the *Rhinoplax vigil,* on the other hand, is solid enough to provide a tombstone-shaped slab of hard yellow material, edged with red at the sides. Its consistency is like that of ivory, its colors so attractive that from time immemorial it has been sought for by Dyak, Malay, and Chinese craftsmen to make carvings.

The legend of the hoopoes, who asked King Solomon for crowns of gold, and then found everyone wanted to exterminate them for their beautiful ornaments, has come true in the case of the hornbill. The Punans not only shot it while roosting or flying, they also felled the tree in which its mate and young ones were immured, and, as the helpless father fluttered around, brought him down as well.

From as early as the sixth century, when a Chinese explorer penned the first hurried brief account of Borneo, the Chinese had come

2. Pliny, *Natural History,* Book 9, Chapter 70.

Chinese rhinoceros horn cup, carved with dragons in relief. Chinese carved wood stand, nineteenth century. *Courtesy Victoria and Albert Museum, London, England.*

Chinese rhinoceros horn goblet, carved in the shape of a lotus, late eighteenth century. *Courtesy Victoria and Albert Museum, London, England.*

in contact with the Dyaks, who regarded the helmet hornbill as the symbol of power and virility and made from its casque beautiful ornaments. These include ear ornaments slipped through a hole in the ear or suspended from it, belt toggles, and sword fittings.

The nearest the Chinese could get to pronouncing the Malay traders' word for hornbill, *gading,* or ivory, was ho-ting. This was written with two Chinese characters meaning "crane's beak." If anything could enhance the status of this exotic in Chinese eyes it was its association with the crane, the symbol of immortality. It was given another fancy name "gold jade," which must have also helped sales a good deal.

By the thirteenth century hornbill was already so well known to the Chinese that writers on connoisseurship were warning their readers always to look out for the wavy, erratic lines of the genuine article, because therc were so many forgeries about. In 1371 a Sultan of Brunei, in Borneo, acknowledged the overlordship of the Chinese Emperor and sent him products of the jungle such as camphor, sweet wood, rattan, gold, honey, birds' nests, rhinoceros horn, and *ho-ting*. The Chinese tribute officials reckoned that a single piece of hornbill ivory with the red sheathing showing on both sides was equivalent to a thousand cash, half an ounce of the best coral beads, or one fifth of an ounce of seed pearls.

The Ming craftsmen worked hornbill ivory into plaques for belts (where its potent effect would be able to make itself felt conveniently near the lumbar regions). Under the Manchu dynasty of Ching which succeeded the Mings, hornbill was used to make belt buckles, archer's thumb rings, tiny figurines, plume holders for holding the feathers on Mandarins' hats, hair ornaments, and above all snuffbottles.

The snuffbottle was the Chinese equivalent of a snuffbox. It was forced on the Chinese because, unlike the Scots, they had been unable to perfect a snuffbox with interior hinges which would not clog up with the snuff. Futhermore, to take snuff with your fingers before inhaling it (as the Europeans did) would stain the long fingernails of which every Manchu gentleman was so proud. A small spoon was necessary to convey the snuff to the nostrils, yet where could you keep a spoon in a box? A bottle was the answer to the problem, with the spoon permanently implanted in the stopper.

Chinese snuff bottle of buffalo horn. Eighteenth or nineteenth century. ***Courtesy Christies, London, England.***

Hornbill ivory was an ideal material for snuffbottles. It was light, it was odorless, and it was extremely expensive and rare. The casque of the hornbill was sawn into three parallel slices, which would make three rather thin bottles. The red sheathing at the side of the casque was preserved and incorporated into the design at the sides of the bottle in the form of ornamental handles or masks. Many prerogatives, bearable when exercised by the aristocratic few, become intolerable when the property of the public as a whole. The demands for hornbill from Manchu China could not have been very great. Today, since Chinese snuffbottles have become a fashionable collecting craze, regular shipments of hornbill are reaching Hong Kong, and even, it is rumored, mainland China, shipments which indicate wholesale slaughter in the jungle. It has been suggested that hornbills are now being bred for their casques in Borneo. This seems un-

Chinese hornbill snuffbottle, carved in relief, depicting on the front a shepherd dozing beneath a pine, while his three sheep keep an eye on him, and on the back twin inscriptions. One, in broadly incised archaic script, the other explaining the first and reading: "Chin-yuan made this *tsun* for the treasured use of Kao-yung." Made in the Tao-kuang period, 1820–1851, this bottle is signed by the seal of *Pai-shih,* an eminent hornbill carver of the early nineteenth century. *Courtesy Hugh M. Moss Limited.*

Chinese hornbill snuffbottle, made between 1780 and 1880. It is carved in relief with a maiden Immortal and *hsieh-chai* on a rocky outcrop. Beneath are the sun and clouds. On the back is a carp rising from the waves and evoking from its mouth a cloud on which sits a pavilion. The sides are carved with a writhing hydra with part of the red sheath of the bill left showing. *Courtesy Hugh M. Moss Limited.*

Chinese hornbill snuffbottle. It is plain on both sides and is carved on the shoulders with masks and imitation ring handles. Made in the twentieth century. *Courtesy Hugh M. Moss Limited.*

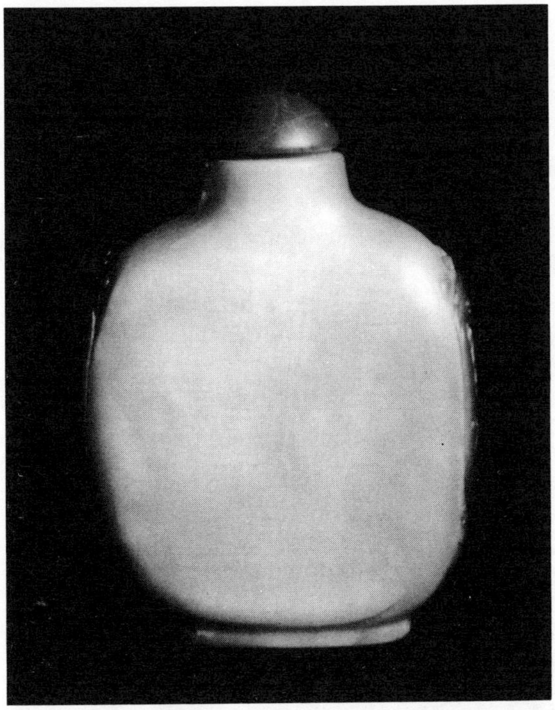

Chinese snuffbottle carved from hornbill. It is plain on both sides and is carved on the shoulders with a representation of a mythological animal. It probably dates from between 1820 and 1880. ***Courtesy Hugh M. Moss Limited.***

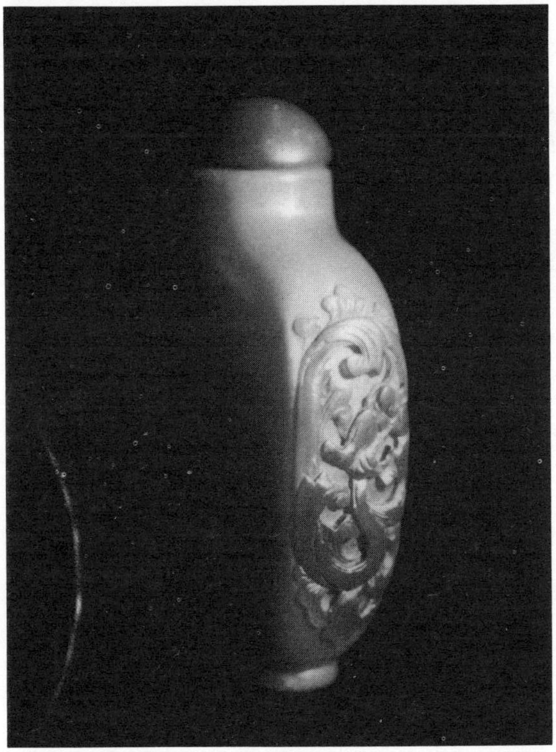

Another view of the same bottle. *Courtesy Hugh M. Moss Limited.*

likely because the breeding habits of the hornbill make the possession of a whole tree by the female necessary. What is more likely is that the poor Bird with the Golden Crown now faces extermination.

In workshops in Hongkong, carvers, who also work at ivory carving, labor at the snuff bottles, making one or two a month. They carve them with the regular set of tools of the Chinese ivory worker, tools which appear crude at first sight, and polish them with carborundum and metal polish. The workmen usually sleep in the atelier, or, if they sleep outside, the proprietor sleeps in. They earn $80 a month if they are fully fledged craftsmen who have been trained for two or three years.

Rhinoceros horn, although no longer carved, is still very much in demand as an aphrodisiac, and it fetches $7.20 an ounce. Rhinoceros horns can be seen sticking out of the counter of the national medicine shops in Hong Kong. If these factors continue to operate, we may well see carvings in hornbill and rhinoceros horn rocket in price as the supplies of the natural materials from which they are made diminish.

The Chinese were just as adept at working the humbler kind of horns as they were those of the rhinoceros or the hornbill. The horns of water buffalo and oxen, and even their hooves, as well as those of other animals, were made into lanterns, which were often elaborately ornamented, and into a variety of other trinkets, including snuffbottles. The lanterns, which were quite transparent, and often of strikingly large size, were made by boiling down the horns of sheep and goats until the different layers of the horn began to separate. Then the layers were parted by means of a sharp tool, and thrown into a pan till they became soft and transparent. Then they were put into a special press, made from hard wood and pre-heated metal plates, which squeezed out completed sections of the lantern. Once these sections had dried and cooled off in the press, they were permanently fixed in their new shape. All that needed to be done to assemble the whole lantern was to trim the edges of the sections with a metal rasp and weld them at the seams by wetting them and pressing them with a hot iron.

Chinese figure of Kuan Yin on the waves, carved in rhinoceros horn. Seventeenth or eighteenth century. ***Courtesy Victoria and Albert Museum, London, England.***

This amalgamated the horn edges which touched one another. The completed lantern was given a polish with a mixture of lime and coal dust spread on a woolen rag.

Bone carving had gotten off to a good start in China through its employment for the bone oracle tablets consulted during the Shang Yin dynasty, in the eighteenth century B.C. These tablets were made from the shoulder plates of cattle; holes were bored through them, and a red hot bronze poker applied to the hole, producing a series of cracks right through the bone. The side of the tablet opposite to the place where the poker had

Fragment of Shang-yin oracle bone.

Modern Chinese character, "bu," meaning "to divine."

been applied was then carefully examined. What the crack lines on it looked like can be seen by looking at the Chinese character for the word "to divine." Depending on the length of the lines, and their relationship to one another, the augurs who examined the bone tablets drew favorable or unfavorable replies, and their interpretations and questions were inscribed on the tablet in a special script with a pointed bronze stylus. Apparently this was a special hieratic script evolved by the augurs, who had great power in the state, just as the Egyptian priests evolved their sacred writing of hieroglyphs. It is difficult to prove this, because the "Shell and Bone Characters," as the Chinese call this style of writing, have not been found on any other writing material. What can be said is that the task of inscribing the script on bone helped to formulate its shape and eventually consolidate all written Chinese. As inscribed on the many bones which have been found at Anyang it is extremely angular, ideally suitable in form to being scratched upon a bone. It must have been a very different script when in its previous form (no relics of which have come down to us) it was drawn with a crude reed pen. Even when the Chinese adopted the brush, a stage which was reached when the oracle bones were still in use, the new written characters were still so like the old inscribed ones that it is usually possible to tell what any engraved character means by looking at its written equivalent.

Recent innovations in written Chinese have taken us rather back towards the old "Shell and Bone" characters, and of all the forms which the written lanquage has gone through they are, to the Westerner, still the most artistic. One reason for this is that they were nearer to the original idea portrayed; the charter for "sun" still looks like the sun, and so forth. Another is that the use of the brush cramped the forms of the written language very much. The number of different shaped strokes which can be drawn (or are allowed to be drawn) in modern written Chinese has been put at eight. The number of curves and lines which could be performed with a metal stylus is almost infinite. As they stand, each character in the "Shell and Bone" style is a complete abstract picture. The Chinese themselves are as aware of the script's beauty as anyone else, and many modern calligraphers still write studio texts in the old character.

Compared with the pulsating beauty of the script in which they were written, the questions and answers inscribed on the oracle bones seem more than a little prosaic. No questioner inquired of the spirits what the next world was like, though they were better equipped to answer that question than any other. Instead they were asked what the weather would be, how the crops would fare, which were lucky days for hunting, journeys, and warfare, and about the outcome and cure of illnesses. King Ling of Chu (540-529 B.C.) asked for the dominion of the world. When the reply was unfavorable, he dashed down the oracle tablet and cried: "What, deny me a little thing like that! I shall take it

Chinese wedding junk, dated about 1800, starboard view. *Courtesy Victoria and Albert Museum, London, England.*

The same junk, forecastle and port view. *Courtesy Victoria and Albert Museum, London, England.*

myself." Another monarch, possibly with his tongue figuratively as well as literally in his cheek, asked which of his ancestors it was who had decided to plague him with the toothache.

Long after the oracle bones had fallen into disuse, bone continued to be used in China for many styles of carvings. They included cricket cages, made from pieces of solid bone sawn into bars with a piercing saw, and fitted with tops equipped with a turned thread which could be securely screwed to the rest of the box and prevent the little prisoner escaping. These were intended to allow cricket fanciers to carry their pets with them in their sleeves. The same kind of craftsmen who did such fine work with a piercing saw may have made the beautiful "wedding junks," and the palace and temple models. A typical wedding junk will contain a crew of the bride and groom, priest and relations, servants, and wedding breakfast, together with tablets bearing characters expressing the wish for a large family for the happy couple. The principal features of the decoration of these models are very thin sheets of bone (and in some cases ivory) sawn into the most elaborate pierced work designs, which recall both the *mosaique* of Dieppe and the pierced work pen trimmers of Turkish carvers. All these models appear to express some sort of wish for a large family. One on display in the *Musée Guimet* in Paris has a tablet in the middle of the courtyard of the model bearing the name of a Chinese legendary figure well known for the number of his children. The most famous of these models is of course the one sent by Napoleon as a present to Josephine. It was captured at sea by the British on its way from the maker, in China, to the court at Paris. At the Peace of Amiens the British government offered it back to Josephine, but Napoleon refused to let her accept this lucky wish for a family. As the Chinese would say: "no catchee luck that way." Soon Napoleon's lack of an heir was going to bring about his downfall, while his marriage with Josephine, once so happy, ended in disaster.

Though a richer country than China, Japan's trade with other nations was restricted. She found it difficult to import exotics such as hornbill ivory and rhinoceros horn, and her craftsmen found themselves obliged to work in much humbler materials. They also tended to work in a much more restricted field. The *netsuke,* a toggle suspending from the girdle on a pendant silk cord which held boxes containing everyday personal possessions such as medicines, a pipe and tobacco, a seal and so forth, was only as big as a good sized walnut.

It was characteristic of the Japanese craftsmen that not only did they enhance and glamourize the humble materials in which they worked, but they showed an amazing ingenuity in being great in little things, and working within the tiny compass of a *netsuke.*

Easily the favorite animal material for *Netsukes* was buckshorn, which was obtained from stags of the Sika deer. Buckshorn was regarded as a specific against snakebite, and a patron who ordered a buckshorn *netsuke* might stipulate that one corner of it was to be left rough, so that a dose of horn shavings could be scraped off if required. The fervent Buddhism of the Japanese had not prevented them from hunting deer, and both the antlers of hunted deer and those shed seasonally were available. Hooves of deer, almost certainly a trophy of the chase, were also used occasionally. Buckshorn is an attractive substance with a creamy light brown color flecked with darker marks and a good dense texture that favors carving. Although wild deer horns often show a good thickness, particularly those from virgin does, who put into the horn the calcium they would otherwise feed out in milk to a suckling fawn, there is always a spongy interior to the antler, which is not really horn, but a kind of bone.

Deer had symbolic associations; they were one of the signs of the Zodiac, and someone born under the sign of the Deer might want to wear a buckshorn *netsuke.* They were associated with Autumn, together with maples, and deer in the mountains recalled the gods of good fortune, Jurojin and Fukurokuju. To the devout Buddhist, the deer, treading along its lonely path, was a symbol of the believer walking through this world of trouble and temptation, swerving neither to right or left, but following the narrow way of righteousness. Buddha had been reborn as a deer many times, and had even taught in this form. Moreover the Chinese word for deer, *"lu"* was identical in sound with the word for "good fortune." Deer symbolized longevity because they were believed to live to a very great age.

Carvers of *netsuke,* such as the Asakusa school, showed the greatest ingenuity in getting the best from buckshorn, while avoiding its more awkward qualities. They would carve striking narrative scenes, such as the fight between those two legendary heros, Benkei and Yoshitsune, out of a single joint of antler, using the nodules on the outside to help out the carving. Particularly famous for their buckshorn *netsuke* were Shogetsu and Ryukoku, together with Kokusai, the most able of the trio, all of whom worked in the nineteenth century.

Like the deer, the ox was a Zodiacal sign. It was the steed of the gods, such as Daikoku, the god of wealth. It was also associated with one of the great heroes of Japan, Sugawara Michizane, who had ridden off into exile on an ox. Though rejected by some carvers because it might become worm eaten, buffalo horn was widely used by others, particularly for the rings which lined the hole through which the cord attached to a *netsuke* passed. Often horn was used, not as a basic material, but as part of the inlay. Toyomasa (1773—1856) was famous for the *netsukes* which he carved at Tamba. They were minute animals of wood, with inlaid eyes of clear horn.

Black and yellow oxhorn and antelope horn were also worked, as were ox and horse thigh bones or shank bones. Any hollow ends which showed up on these bones were plugged with other pieces of bone. Two well known carvers of the nineteenth century, Gemmin and Tsuzen, both specialized in this material.

No aspect of bone carving, anywhere in the world, was more extraordinary than its employment in Tibet for a variety of carvings made from human bone. No grave gaped for the dead Tibetan; instead his corpse was carried to some mountainside and dismembered by the disposers of the dead. Although birds and wild animals picked up most of the fragments, there were always enough human bones to supply raw material for carvings. From these relics Black Hat lamas would select thigh bones (preferably belonging to a criminal, or someone who had died a violent death). After weird rites, these would be handed to a craftsman who would carve trumpets from them, sheathed in brass and provided with a wide copper bell mouth. On this were figured the three eyes and the nose of a demon, the opening of the trumpet itself being the demon's mouth. The thigh bone trumpet was one of the symbols of the Tibetan religious life. When the patron deity of Sikkim, Lha Tsun, called on the Dalai Lama in 1648, he announced his presence by blowing on just such a trumpet.

Another musical instrument played upon by lamas and made from human bones was a small rattle hand drum shaped like a large double egg-cup. It was made from two skull caps. Other religious uses for human bones were to make the sashes of bone plaques depicting fiends and mystic symbols worn by the sorcerers of the Black Hat sect. Rosaries made from discs cut from human skulls were used in the worship of the dead. Much more secular were the beautiful chess sets carved from human bone. They were perforated so that they could hang on pegs on the wall, instead of being set on a board. The shapes of the individual men are some of the most striking designs for gaming pieces ever made. Other bone and horn carving was done in Tibet and beautifully carved horns, ornamented with scorpions and other symbols, served as containers to hold the charmed seeds or pebbles thrown at demons.

11

BARBARIC BONE

Primitive Carving

PRIMITIVE bone carving inspired that which was carried out in more settled societies. Chinese hornbill carvers, for example, may have been encouraged to carve the wonderful belt plaques which Ming courtiers wore on the large hoops of stiffened leather which formed part of their official dress, by the beautiful belt or sword toggles which the Dayaks made from the same material.

It was all the more unfortunate that many schools of primitive carving died out in isolation and left no cultural inheritors. They include the Mixtecs, who carved jaguar bones into wonderful low relief spatulas, depicting animals, chiefs and calendar signs. Some spatulas were enriched with turquoise mosaic, an art which wandered as far north as New Mexico, where the Pueblo people made bone pendants inlaid with jet and turquoise.

In Peru, bone spatulas were also made at Mochicha. These were shaped like a human arm and scrimshawed with fantastic figures of men dressed as birds and inlaid with turquoises and iron pyrites.

Although most Indians north of the Rio Grande carved some bone, such as the elk tusk embellishments worn by Plains Indian women or the bone pendants which Beothuk squaws sewed to the hem of their clothes, really fine bone carvings were only made on the Pacific coast. The beautifully carved ornaments, weapons, totems, and utensils, often enriched with abalone shell inlay, are among the finest products of any Indian culture.

The Haida and Tlingit Indians, who produced the best carvings, had whalebone and other bones in abundance. They were also in touch with the Eskimos and learned from them something of their peculiar deftness in bone carving. The masks carved on the whalebone war clubs used on the Pacific coast recall those carved by the Eskimos on their harpoon line runners. These clubs were decorated with beautiful chip carving on the shaft, and an eagle beak carved on the handle.

Chip carving also adorned the ladles carved by the tribes from big-horn sheep horns, while Pacific carving rises to its greatest heights in the horn spoons carved on the back with stylized patterns representing hawks, killer whales, beaver, and sea monsters, and in similarly decorated horn bowls. The symbolic designs which adorn these carvings adapt well to the tough,

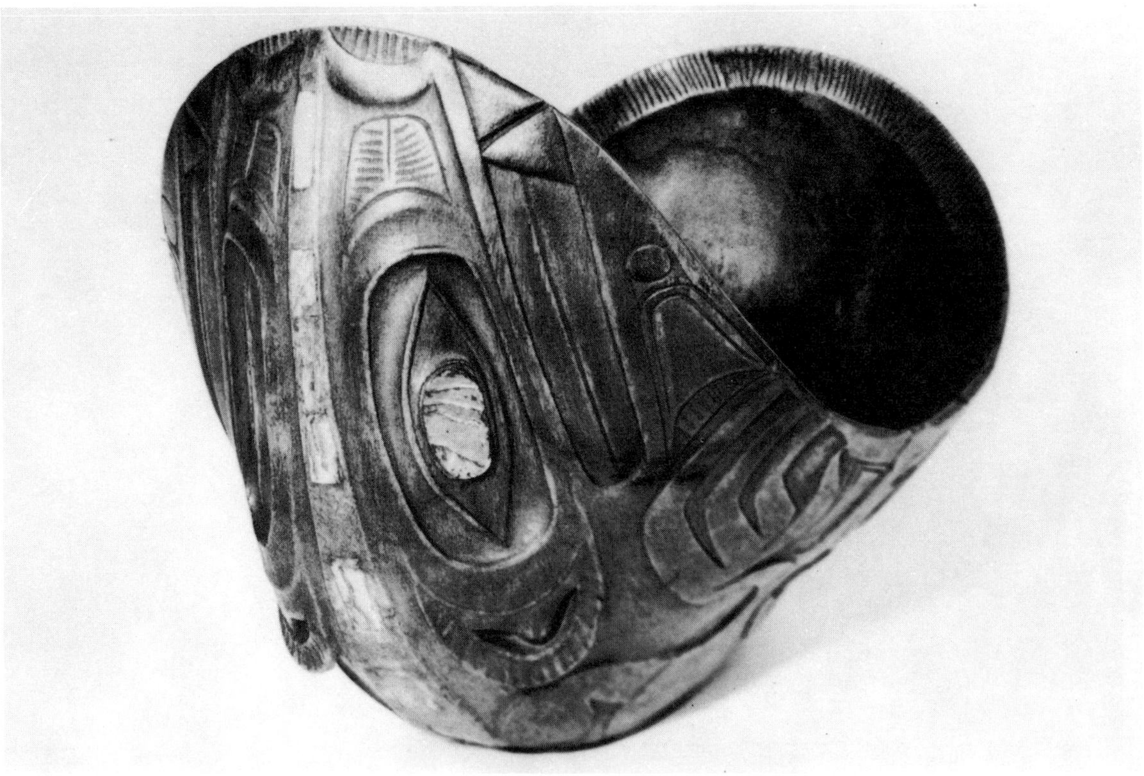

Carved elk horn bowl inset with abalone decoration. Northwest Pacific Coast, North America. *Courtesy Horniman Museum, London, England.*

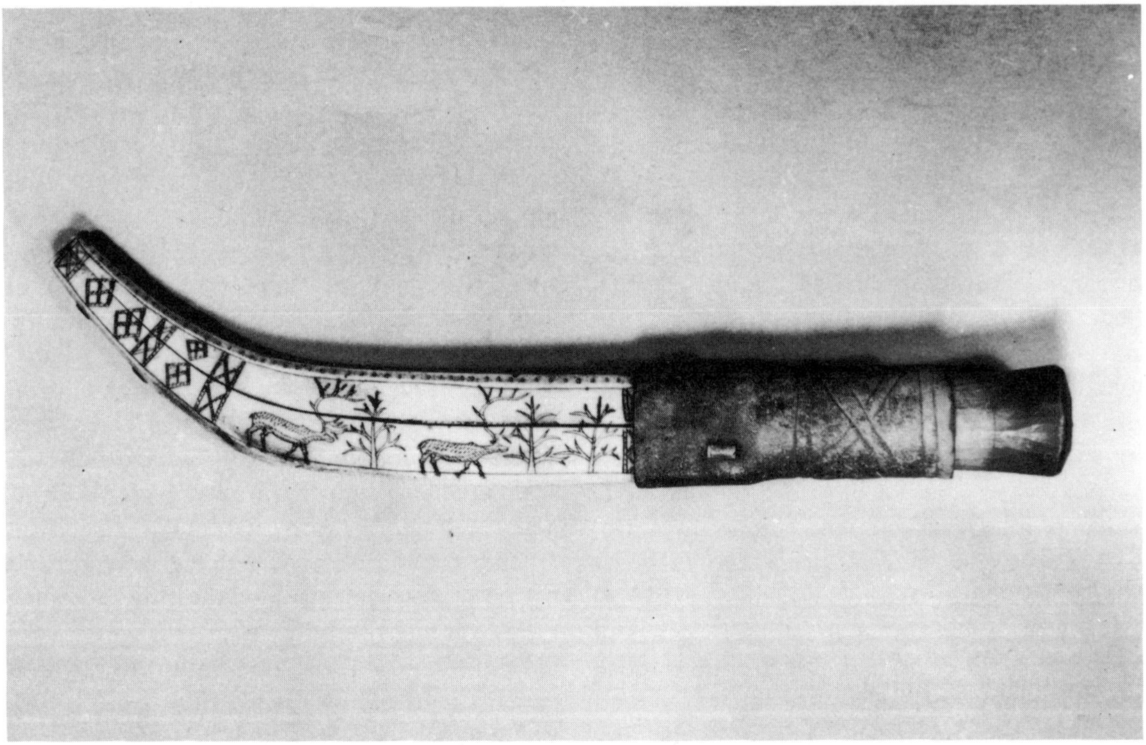

Two views of a Lapp knife sheath, probably nineteenth century. The Lapps, who still carry scrimshawed knives and herdsmen's sticks, may have been introduced to bone carving by the Vikings. *Courtesy Horniman Museum, London, England.*

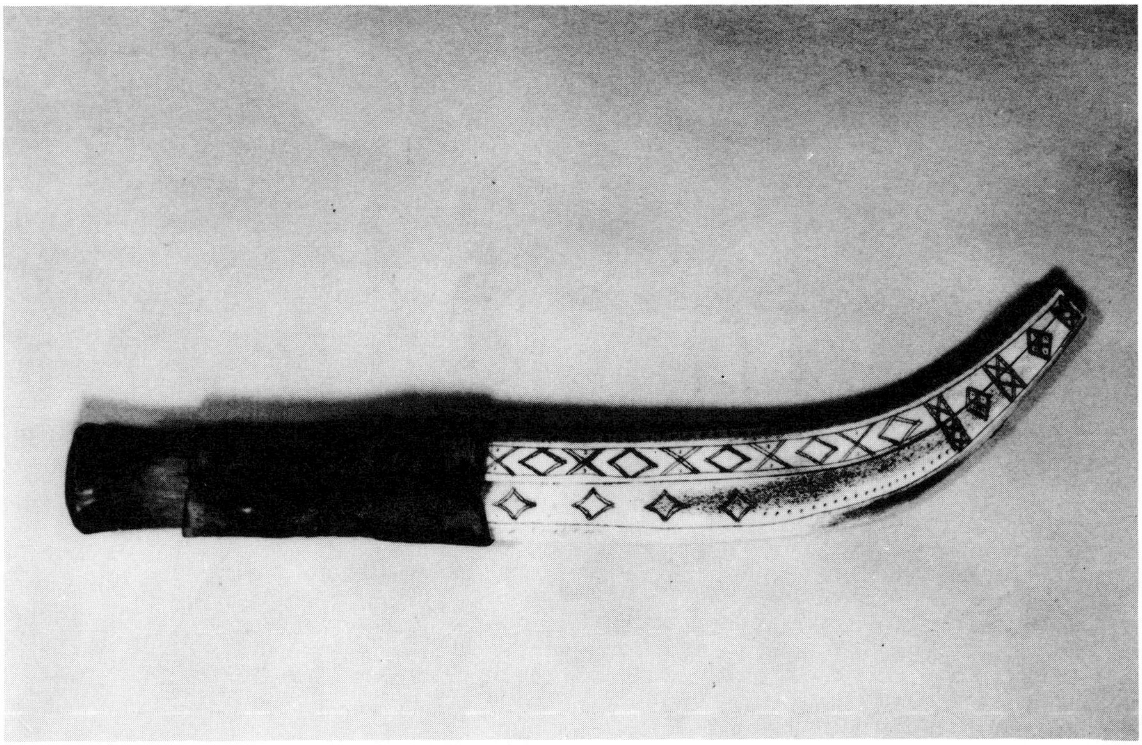

The other side of the Lapp knife sheath. *Courtesy Horniman Museum, London, England.*

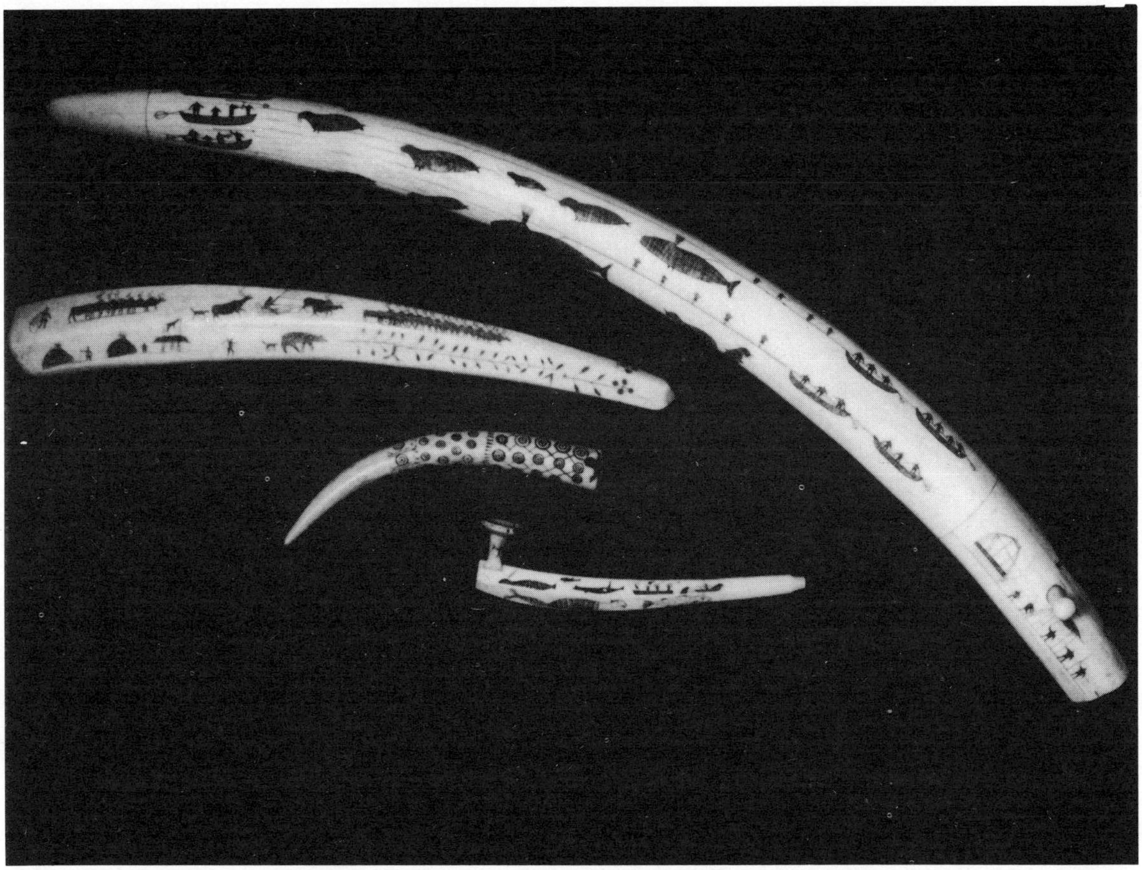

Antler and ivory Eskimo scrimshaw. *Courtesy Horniman Museum, London, England.*

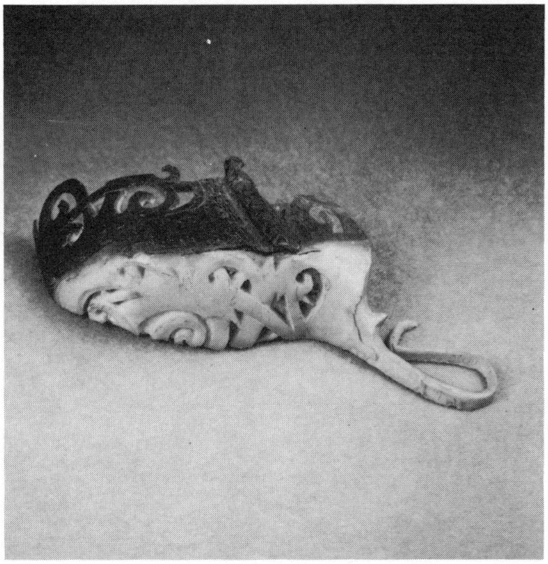

Native jewelry from Sarawak, man's earring made from hornbill. *Courtesy Commonwealth Institute.*

close grained material, a substance carved, apparently effortlessly, with very simple tools: stone knives, scrapers, saws, drills and grinders.

In Arctic America an abundant supply of raw material, the frequent absence of competitive materials such as wood, a millennia-old bone carving tradition, the need to make essential tools and weapons from bone, and the sacred attributes of the material, which was used by the shaman to make his magic implements, all contributed to produce bone carvings of great distinction.

The Eskimos seem to have inherited from Stone Age folk their talent for bone carving, along with other cultural attributes that have been already mentioned. Both peoples had a lot in common, including an abundance of game. The great Eskimo civilizations of early times developed in association with an ample food supply which allowed leisure time to be devoted to art. At Okvik, on the island of St. Lawrence, south of the Bering Straits, where great droves of walrus were hunted along the shores, a famous school of bone carving arose between 300 B.C. and 100 A.D. The Old Bering Sea and Punuk cultures, which succeeded Okvik, also had a good food supply, from whaling. They produced beautifully scrimshawed weapons and carvings. The Ipiutak people, who lived on the American shore of the Bering Straits between the start of the Christian Era and about 500 A.D., were mighty hunters, migrating from their caribou ranges in the interior to their seal hunting grounds on the coast.

In more recent times the Aleut tribes of Eskimos, the Alaskans, and the Dorset men of Greenland, migrants from America, raised bone carving to heights which were significant, not just from the point of view of Eskimo art, but from that of world art as a whole. Eskimo carving has left a permanent impress upon modern sculpture. To take a random example, the technique of carving multiple faces evolved by Jan Holschuh probably owes a good deal to Eskimo inspiration.

To tackle an apparently intractable material the Eskimo developed all sorts of ingenious devices. They used for their carvings stone adzes, "crooked knives" of chipped flint or obsidian, set with multiple small flakes of flint set in a wooden or bone handle, thong drills, which one craftsman held in place and another revolved by means of a twisted thong, bow drills, which one craftsman could work for himself by holding the end of the drill shaft between his teeth while he held the work to be drilled with one hand and used the bow with the other, flint scrapers, stone rubbers of andesitic lava or tuff, and a plant called horse tail (*equisetum nyemale*) which imparted the final polish to bone carvings.

The carver began work, long before he actually picked up his tools, by pickling the bone or horn that was to be carved in urine. When the bone had absorbed so much liquid that it would carve easily, the sculptor cut it down to the size he wanted by sawing a deep groove round the section of the bone to be carved, and breaking off the piece required with a blow from a hammer stone. Next he cut a groove along the top of the block which he had obtained and hammered in a bone wedge till he had split the block in two. Further wedging and splitting reduced the piece to exactly the size required. The bone was now shaped with chisels and gouges made of flint blades held in wooden handles. A sharp splinter of quartz held in a wooden handle produced the wonderful Eskimo scrimshaw. Possibly it was two such splinters, teamed up on one tool, which cut the double lines characteristic of much Eskimo work. Small stone knives, and possibly other tools as well, such as beaver teeth, helped with fine carving. Once finished a carving would be polished with natural abrasives, such as powdered lava, followed by powdered tuff, and then the horsetail already mentioned.

Innumerable tools and pieces of equipment, such as wild fowlers' snares, scrapers for removing snow from kayak decks, bows, sledges, tent poles (made from the penis bones of walruses) were fabricated from bone and horn. Whale bones held up the Eskimo house roof, and the kayak was put together with innumerable pieces of bone, such as the studs on the deck to which hunting weapons were fastened.

The Eskimo had no conception of fine art, as we know it. Scrimshaw itself, the most characteristic of Eskimo decorative styles, may have been adopted originally to prevent bone weapons warping towards the side of least density, or to give a firm grip to the holder. Everything that was not practical was magical. When an Aleut drew a pattern consisting of five parallel lines with spots in the middle of them, and other lines branching off to the side, the whole design probably represented the spine and flippers of a walrus or seal, and was thus an unspoken prayer for good hunting.

Statuettes of men, women and animals were fetishes or amulets rather than studio pieces. Even devices which appear to be purely decorative usually have some religious association. For example, the bone silhouette cut-out figures used to ornament wooden objects, such as spear throwers, kayak paddles, knife handles, and so forth, which seem so conventionalized as to be abstract, are really the highly stylized representations of animals, or mythological beings, and are intended to implore protection while hunting on sea or land.

These silhouettes are among the most pleasing objects in Eskimo bone carving. They include mythological beings such as *tornarsuks,* narwhals, whales, bears, birds, fish, men, and kayaks. Often a realistic design has become completely conventionalized and has to be explained by the artist to be understood. An hourglass figure represents a seal, for example.

Whatever objects the bone carver took in hand he enhanced, and the beads, earrings, needle cases, bone combs, carved drumsticks and buttons which he made are among the most entrancing objects in primitive art.

12
ENVOI

IT is no cheering task to chronicle the final age of horn and bone. Both substances are still being worked, but on a more and more utilitarian level. The invention by Lynn in 1828 of the twinning machine, which cut two combs out of one plate of horn, spelled the destruction of comb making as a craft industry. Other inventions followed; they included ram and wedge presses, screw presses, hydraulic presses for molding patterns on combs, circular saws for slitting the horns, special furnaces for softening them, and so forth.

The transition from craft worker to factory hand can be seen in the transformation of the old fashioned Scottish "horner" into the employees of Stewart, Rowell, and Co., who opened their combworks at Aberdeen, Scotland, in 1830. "In the habit of working irregularly at home, like tailors," said a director of the firm in 1851, "they disliked our systematised division of labor; they resisted, rebelled, and left their work on more than one occasion when they knew we required them most. We shewed them the necessity of consistent labor for ten hours a day six days in the week. We reasoned with them, but never coerced. At this moment we have infinitely less trouble in managing 600 people than we had at one time in managing fifty."[1]

By 1851 almost everything in the Stewart and Rowell works was done by machinery. Only the finishers, who persisted in calling themselves "the combmakers" so as to distinguish themselves from the machine tool workers, continued to carry out handwork, carving elaborate chain ornament on braid combs.

This decline in craftsmanship had become characteristic of horn and bone carving in most other parts of Europe at about the same time. Russian bone carving, the *Archangel Provincial News* complained in 1868, was almost extinct.[2] However in Russia "bone carving" has a particular and rather misleading meaning. It refers to carving done in fossil mammoth tusk. Why this should be is something of a mystery. There is a perfectly good Russian word meaning "ivory," and another meaning "bone." However ivory is not really a proletarian sounding material, nor did the great Russian "bone carvers" labor for the people, but rather for the nobility and the Czar, who sent magnificent carvings like Nikolay Vereschagin's vases as presents to foreign potentates, like the Shogun of Japan. Kholmogory ivory carvers are still at work, trying "to reflect life as it is today, and first of all in the North."[3] This aspiration, as interpreted by a carver like Sharypina-Tryapitsina, means carving four

1. *Chambers Edinburgh Journal* Vol. XVI (Edinburgh: William and Robert Chambers, 1852), p. 70.

2. Y. Ousyannikov, *Russian Folk Art Carvings.*

3. Ibid.

Although some Russian carvings, such as this superb vase by Nikolay Stephanovich Vereschagin (1770–c. 1814) are often labeled "bone carvings," they are in reality carvings made from mammoth ivory dug out of the frozen tundra in Siberia. Ivan Vereschagin, the descendant of Nikolay, is still carving in Kholmogory, but the stock of mammoth ivory is almost exhausted. *Courtesy State Art Collections, Moscow.*

Pierre Graillon, nineteenth-century Dieppe carver, made many carvings, working in whalebone, ivory, and other materials. ***Courtesy Dieppe Museum, photographed by Delacroix and Poidvin, Dieppe.***

foxes chasing two squirrels in a field of Dieppe-type *mosaique,* all in walrus ivory and very attractive.

True bone carving in Russian started in 1946, when the Council of Ministers of the Russian Federation decided to set up a bone carving center at Khotkovo, a small town near Moscow. The carvers were to be trained, not by the ivory carvers of Kholmogory, but by boxwood carvers from Zagorsk. Dentists drills were installed in the carving factory, and work began. Buttons and jewelry were

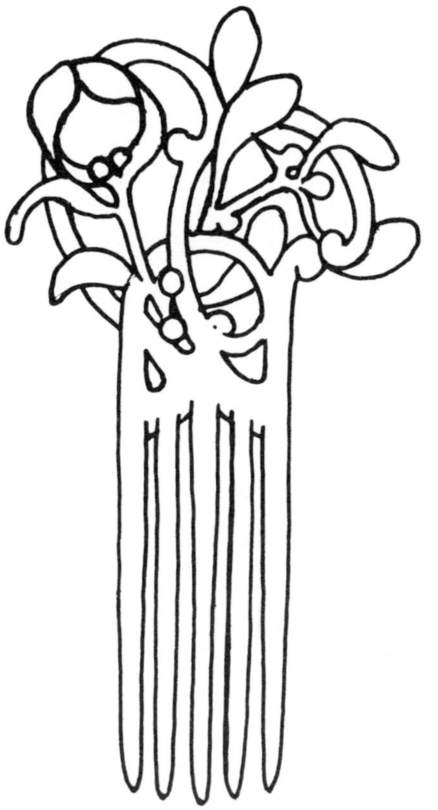

Comb of horn, gold, and pearls, Art Nouveau period.

made, inspired by natural objects, but the carvers, men like Vladimir Loginov, Fyodor Mozikov, Vasily Kalmykov and others found it difficult to get a wide range of sculptured objects out of the material available—plates of beefbones five or six millimeters thick. The factory has now returned to making animals in boxwood.

Horn carving was started as a side industry of the Mikoyan Meat Packing plant in 1952, two sausage makers and a graduate of Moscow Industrial Art College spearheading the project. Using dentist's drill and rotary files of different shapes, carvers such as Victor Kuznetsov turn out horn animals, such as seals, which are not without their charm. Sluvis Urtayeva, another of the carvers, admits to being inspired by one of the indigenous arts of Russia, Chukotka carving, which set him on to carving his first seal. More talent of the indigenous folk colonized by Russia is being tapped in the bone carving centers in Buryat, Mongolia, and Altai, and among the Yakuts, who probably did a lot to inspire the start of Russian ivory carving.

By contrast with Russian carving, where even the polish is put on the horn by machinery, the work of modern Lapp craftsmen such as Esaias Poggats, who makes utensils of birch and horn, seems very handmade indeed. The Lapps are inheritors of a very old tradition of horn engraving which appears to be related both to Eskimo and to American scrimshaw.

Other Scandinavian countries have thriving schools of bone and horn carving, such as Denmark, where Erland Borglund and Jacob Flauensgaard are at work, producing charming jewelry, cutlery, and other craft pieces, and the Faeroes, where beautiful knife handles of baleen, inlaid with silver, are still made.

Apart from these craftsmen, who have been taught in art colleges, there are very many untutored horn and bone workers all over the world, from Rhodesia, where you can see horn carvers selling their wares by the roadside, to Java, where until very recently a strong local school, concerned with comb making, was in being. An examination of a Javanese horn worker's work methods is illuminating, in that it reveals the very many processes necessary from splitting the raw horn to polishing the finished comb. Folk craftsmen such as the comb maker cannot long continue to ply their trades. In the face of competition from plastics issuing from the new industrial centers of the Far East their wares are invariably over-priced, so far as the consumer is concerned. The time is not far off when the last hornworker will lay aside his tools, and man's oldest art will have reached the end of its history.

INDEX